# MENTAL TOUGHNESS

THE ABILITY TO MOVE FORWARD UNDER PRESSURE

COACH P - JIM PUSATERI

# DEDICATION

*This book is dedicated to many in my life who left this world way too early. Especially my sons, John (age 26, 2007) and Joe (age 28, 2019). May you all rest in peace.*

# TABLE OF CONTENTS

# A PREFACE TO MENTAL TOUGHNESS

I cannot believe that this book has finally made it to print. It's been part of my goals for at least 10 years now. During one of my times of reflection, I pondered why I have seen, and endured so much death and grief in my life. It struck me that maybe I am here to help others through tough times. I guess that's why I'm getting so much experience so I can share these life lessons with others. Thus starts the beginning of my Mental Toughness journey. Since that time, I have set out to learn as much as I can regarding what I call Mental Toughness, the ability to MOVE FORWARD under life's pressure.

After 65 years of hard knocks experience, I have come to write this book, develop mental performance training and master classes to help others not make the same mistakes, and also how to deal with the problems of life. I truly believe that life is nothing more than a series of problems, and success is determined by how you handle those problems. You cannot let the problems of your past determine your future. You need to develop a growth mindset, one that allows you to move forward under the toughest circumstances.

I must admit this book is inspired by many people I have come across in my life, the ones who sought out my expertise, but most of all this book is inspired by my inner drive and my passion for mentoring others. Once I found my passion (what makes me tick), I dedicated my life to helping others develop Mental Toughness and the 3 Phases of Achievement so they can live that amazing life everyone is seeking.

This book is so important because everyone experiences death, setbacks, and makes mistakes in life, but most let those setbacks and mistakes frame the rest of their life. This book is here to help you move past those mental blocks and learn how to use the 3 phases of achievement to obtain the success you seek.

I could spend the next 100 pages trying to acknowledge all the people in my life who have help in one way or another and gave me the strength to be able to overcome great obstacles in my life. There are some very special people in my life who I think already know how I feel about them. But I do need to acknowledge my family, my life long friend and wife Cathie, my sons, my grand children those are the ones that keep me going on this journey of life. As you will learn when reading this book, you must have a **WHY** if you want to develop the mental toughness that is needed to overcome life's pressure. Without my family, friends, students, coaches and all the players I have coached I probably would of never reach this stage of my life were I feel the passion, motivation and fulfillment each and every day.

Special shout to Harley Liechty (https://harleywrites.com/). Without his help writing this book, it would probably still be a task on my goal sheet. Remember goals are a lifelong thing, it doesn't matter how long it takes as long as you achieve them.

# CHAPTER 1
# TOO TOUGH TO BE MENTALLY TOUGH?

Mental toughness is a funny thing to write about when you're old. By the time most folks are in their 60s, they are looking at getting relaxed time off and slowing down. When's the next game of golf and the next happy hour, huh? We've worked so hard through our lives just to make it here. We might as well enjoy it while we still can, right?

I guess I see life a little differently than most my age. I remember how many years I worked away to get to this point. I remember the good times, and I remember the many bad times. While it's tempting to see my age and think I can relax, I've gotten wiser than that. I know what it took to get here. I know what I had to go through, and I know I can't stop now.

Once you become genuinely mentally tough, you're always that way. Those of you who know my story, the many friends and family I've gained over the years, have your own stories of triumphs and losses. You know that when you begin to get lethargic about life, life ain't really worth living anymore. Unfortunately, we see it on all the faces of the old folks in their nursing homes. They're just waiting for life to be over!

But for me? I'm not waiting to die. As a mid-60s old man, I still have plenty of years left to live! I've trained myself for over 40 years to become a mentally tough man, a man who takes charge and seizes the dreams that life gives me. There's no way in the world I'd ever let that go. It's been too fun.

I want everyone to become mentally tough, and that's why I wrote this book.

## FIND MENTAL TOUGHNESS IN ALL PARTS OF LIFE

It was well known during his time that Walter Payton, the former Super Bowl champion and offensive player of the year for the Chicago Bears, started every single day with hill sprints. Even in the off-season, you would find "Sweetness" (as he was nicknamed) running up and down an iconic hill in Arlington Heights, Illinois. He ran this hill so frequently that the city named the hill after him.

Hill sprints will not only help you burn more fat and build more muscular legs, but it will push your mental limits to the extreme. Mental toughness was precisely what a record-setting NFL running back, like Walter Payton, needed to be a champion. It's also what he needed to keep his longevity in the game. Over the 13 seasons that Walter Payton played in the NFL, he only missed one game. That's incredible. The average length of a career in the NFL is 3.3 years, and many players leave due to physical injuries.

If you keep reading about Walter Payton's life, you'll find his story to continually look more incredible. The idea of mental toughness started at a very young age for "Sweetness." According to his biography, *Never Die Easy*, his mother was quite the yard keeper. Back when I grew up, in the '50s and '60s, children were used more often as indentured servants for their parents! Parents who had many kids also had lots of help around the house.

For Walter Payton, his labor was moving topsoil across the entire yard. He started at the age of six, moving over a hundred pounds of topsoil all over the yard with his brother. Imagine what this massive, hundred-pound pile of dirt looks like to a seven-year-old! That's twice the weight of a typical seven-year-old!

This very overwhelming task gave Walter a few early lessons about mental toughness. One of those lessons included **simply working at something until completion.** Here's how Walter described the experience:

> *"...That yard work taught me a lot. I learned about working hard and staying with something even though the project seemed overwhelming... You have to imagine how big that huge pile of dirt appeared to a seven-year-old. I used to think we would never finish.* ***We'd just try to make dents in it every day. Which is how you have to approach any kind of work.*** *You have to take things one day at a time... You work as hard as you can for as long as you can and the small gains you make will eventually pay off."*

Another advantage is that Walter Payton started at an early age. Instead of the many 20-somethings today who are very unwilling or able to put in long hours, Walter figured out these skills before he hit puberty. Study after study about mastering skills and childhood development demonstrates that **people have the greatest chance of mastering skills if they start early.** Why do you find most Olympic gymnasts began before they were ten years old!? You see this in a majority of professional sports.

This also fostered Payton's obsession for his main passions, which is a primary requirement for mental toughness. Here's Walter Payton discussing his love for competition and sports:

> *"Competing in sports back then was everything. No matter what the game was or how much older and stronger the other kids were, we were taught to give it everything we had until it was over. Never give less than one hundred percent.* ***If you start something, you shouldn't quit, that is what we were taught.*** *If you're going to play, you might as well play to be your best."*

We read stories from Walter Payton and sit in amazement. This man has been praised repeatedly by NFL all-star running backs, like Emmitt Smith and LaDainian Tomlinson. His name is literally on a trophy awarding the player with the most outstanding mental toughness in a given season (The Walter Payton Award). What stands out about The Walter Payton Award is it extends past the playing field. It's not only awarded to mentally tough playing on the field, but also great achievement in volunteering and charity work in their city's community. This man's legacy and performance on the field will provide you with quite the education!

Can't we find stories like this everywhere, though? Especially if we look at the great athletes who paid top dollar in sports like football, baseball, hockey, or basketball. Don't all of them have mental toughness? There are a lot of great athletes competing in the world. According to the Bureau of Labor statistics, there were 13,600 jobs available for professional athletes in the United States. It doesn't sound like many people, considering the 330 million people who live in the United States. These aren't the only great athletes, however.

Having the mental toughness to excel in college sports is a feat. Then in many high school sports leagues, it's just as competitive as college athletics. In states like Texas, high school games have tens of thousands of fans attending games and very athletic kids tearing each other apart. Even if less than 1% of athletes make it to the professional leagues, **we could easily believe that there are well over half a million athletes who demonstrate mental toughness by excelling in great high school, collegiate, and professional sports.**

Let's broaden our scope of mental toughness. Mothers illustrate mental toughness by persevering through pregnancy. They train disobedient children every day and, more often than not, also work a full-time job. Roofers are mentally tough because they sweat gallons every day in the summer heat and barely have the energy to do anything else. They're often only doing it to provide a better future for their families. MBA students are mentally tough because they need to spend copious amounts of hours studying, and maybe after several years of school, they earn a high-paying dream job. Doctors spend over a decade of schooling, clinical training, and massive debt to save lives and build a future for their families one day. All of these examples require outstanding mental toughness!

Mental toughness is everywhere, and the ideas of building mental toughness are taught in countless books and stories from people's lives. In Dan Miller's book, *48 Days to the Work You Love,* he gives the blueprint to building a successful, mentally tough life. He writes, ***"Success is never an accident.*** *It typically starts as imagination, becomes a dream, stimulates a goal,* *grows into a plan of action—which then inevitably meets with opportunity."*

To make it even more crystal clear…

1. It starts by just asking yourself, "Huh...I wonder if I'd be good at that? What an interesting idea."
2. Then, you think about the idea a lot. It comes up multiple times in discussions, and you receive confirmation from others to pursue it.
3. The thought nags you constantly to take some action finally. You come up with some arbitrary goal to accomplish.
4. To accomplish the goal, you hit the ground running, stumble, fail a lot, and receive helpful feedback from others. So, you can do it!
5. Finally, as Mr. Miller put it, all this work is inevitably met with the opportunity to accomplish more in areas you couldn't have imagined were possible initially.

Simple, right?

## 60 YEARS LATER, I'M FINALLY MENTALLY TOUGH

Well, it wasn't so simple for me. It sounds too simple to be true for many of you reading this book! Sure, you see Walter Payton, LeBron James, Elon Musk, and countless esteemed people doing extraordinary things. But you're not one of those people. You live an everyday life with routine problems. These greats have trouble dealing with too many fans while you're just having a rough time affording high gas prices.

Yeah, Stephen Curry slaved away practicing his 3-pointers, but you're just trying to find a job that pays you a living wage!

It looked impossible for me too, and it didn't seem probable for a long time! I had many tragic deaths happen throughout my life. My younger brother died when I was only 28 years old, and his passing still eats at me. I had missed job opportunities, debilitating addictions that cost me relationships, and financial stress. I basically had to start over financially after the 2008 recession!

I didn't even know my actual goals and passions until I was 56 years old! The housing markets crashed in 2008, and I lost everything. This was a time when many people started over in their careers and financial positions. I had multiple businesses, was a thriving head football coach, and even gotten back to school to officially get a bachelor's degree. And what happened to me? I lost my businesses and had to take a job selling equipment at a sporting goods store. It really could have been rock bottom for me. I'm getting closer to being called "old" and now working a job a 19-year-old kid could do? Why couldn't I get a solid foot on the ground? Will this indeed be my entire life?

By the time the 2008 recession hit, I had read many of our age's thought-provoking and time-tested books. I had learned what it's like to live with mental toughness. I had quit drinking alcohol, been successful in several ways, and knew how to make a life for myself. Why throw in the towel now? I launched back into my bachelor's degree, made the most of my sporting goods job, and after completing my degree at the young age of 56, I moved to Florida to become a football coach and teacher. Sure enough, just two years after graduating with my bachelor's, I became a head football coach and taught business education.

**It took me forty years to figure out my true passions and become a mental toughness nut!** And while this pursuit of a better life has been exhausting at times, it's all worth it. I'll always be happy about life, no matter the issues. I'm living my passions. I've always got goals I'm setting and executing. I have the mindset to keep myself motivated and am encouraged through all the ups and downs life brings.

This is far better than any riches, fame, and material success can provide because all those things can be ripped from you instantly. Mental toughness guarantees that no matter what life throws at you, you're able to handle it like a true professional, just like Walter Payton. Fame and fortune are fleeting endeavors. If that's your ambition in life, you haven't found your real passion. You certainly won't become mentally tough. I believe Dan Sullivan said it best where he instructs us with this: *"Only a small percentage of people are continually successful [in the culturally popular sense] over the long run."*

This book has been an idea of mine for a long time. As my fate has become what I've hoped for, I see people everywhere in my life that aren't living the way I live. They don't feel fulfilled. They aren't driven to reach a goal. They're simply living a safe life. I see teachers who gave up on their dreams and took an easier job with security. I see husbands and wives who lost the flame for each other, and it seems hopeless for a change. You can see it in their faces whenever they're doing their job. There's no spark to their profession! Just a minimal effort to make ends meet.

I want to help teach you how to become mentally tough. If you're a younger man or woman, you're in luck by picking up this book. If I can help you save 40 years of hard-knocks education, you'll live your most fruitful years with a mentally tough mind! For old folks like myself, it's never too late to become mentally tough. You've only got so many years left. Why waste it away like every other old person? We see too many older people stuck inside, watching television, scrolling Facebook, losing friendships every year due to age, and ending life with no adventure. Man, even if I'm able to help one person positively improve, this will all be worth it!

## SADLY, FEW NEVER BECOME MENTALLY TOUGH

Let's just cut to the chase. Very few people will become mentally tough. **The first step in demonstrating mental toughness is to realize that it's a journey only a few people travel.** Here's why:

1.) **Hard thinking is hard.** Building up mental toughness isn't for the faint at heart. We weren't born with it, so it needs to be learned through great honesty and personal reality checks. It takes some serious, hard thinking, and as Martin Luther King Jr. talks about below, that's the very thing few people want to do.

***"Rarely do we find men who willingly engage in hard, solid thinking.*** *There is an almost universal quest for easy answers and half-baked solutions. Nothing pains some people more than having to think."*

**Without mental toughness, you can't think hard about your true passions.** You can't sit down and figure out what you want to be good at or what you're already good at. You'll simply drift around from job to job, hoping to make a livable income and not die. But where is the purpose behind this? Where is your life fulfillment whenever you just simply look to survive? Just to say that you "survived a long time?" Come on!

We, as humans, have a great advantage over any other species by **thinking about how we want to live our lives.** We have creative ideas about life and how we want to live it. Why not figure out how to make that happen?

2.) **It's Easy to Corrupt Our Perception.** Without determining a clear path, we let everyone else tell us what to do. And since most people aren't mentally tough, it corrupts our perception of what we can achieve. Since most people settle and don't fulfill your ambitions, they'll encourage you to settle too. Since most people are angry, disappointed, discouraged, and annoyed by life, they will give you this distorted, twisted view of the world to drag you down.

**Without mental toughness...your perception of the world gets corrupted.** It's the mentally tough individuals who understand that few will follow them. They can understand who the "Wise Willy's" are from the "Lazy Larry's." Even when everyone tells them that it's a pipe dream, they still take action. Even if they don't achieve everything their hearts desire, they can take the good and forget the bad. Perception is a crucial part of mental toughness, and we'll dive into that much more.

3.) **You'll Always Have a Losing Perspective.** It sounds hokey, but it really is true. If you think you'll lose, you probably will lose. If you think you'll win, then even if you lose, you'll still perform better, move on, and improve. I had to learn this through the school of hard knocks, but you don't have to! Keep reading, and you'll see why this straightforward truth has powered the best and brightest (and myself) to keep moving forward.

4.) **Goals Won't Be Achieved, and Progress Won't Be Made.** These three aforementioned reasons create a snowball effect of a lack of productivity, motivation, and the ability to just get through difficult times. Without mental toughness, you won't be able to accomplish the goals you have set for your life!

5.) **Finally, You Can't Persevere Through the Inevitable Ups and Downs.** Everyone has tough times, and everyone falls. How you get up and rebound from adversity matters. Without mental toughness, you have no hope of recovering.

*Without mental toughness, you'll never finish like a champion.*

## THE 5 P'S OF MENTAL TOUGHNESS

So how do we develop mental toughness? It stems from the five P's that I've come up with to guide us on the pathway to fortifying mental toughness. These are five words that capture distinct natures of mental toughness. Each word goes through a mental and practical game we all need to play to guarantee mental toughness in life. We'll dive much more deeply into each one, but let's provide some introductions.

### Passion

It's the few things in life that make you tick. No matter what happens, you always come back to it and wish to return! Passions are activities or interests where, if you had no financial worries or concerns, you would participate for free.

I can't tell you how long it will take to find your passion, but if you never stop pursuing your passions, you will always attain them. I believe it was Zig Ziglar who said: *"Go as far as you can see, and when you get there, you will be able to see farther."* Life is a fun journey if you are chasing your passion. Otherwise, it's just a dead-end job!

We'll walk through how to think about goals and discover passions, but once you find your love, make it your main focus for everything you do in life. This is especially important for the mediocre or negative moments in life. If your passion is genuine and a burning, intense desire, it'll carry you through anything you face in life.

## Perception

Perception is the particular attitude toward how we view something. It's the understanding, labeling, and interpretation we place upon our circumstances. It's how you categorize whether something is good or bad. Is the glass half empty or half full?

Regarding finding "success," that's entirely relative to your goals and how big you dream. You could identify success as making a ton of money. Finding a great spouse and raising a good, loving family is success enough for many people. It could be living in a van down by the river for all I care! People have different perceptions of what qualifies as success.

A great lesson I hope you glean from the book is that **you need to be fully aware of your internal perceptions of the world.** External factors can easily affect your perception, but your inner compass, mindset, and moral views must be strong enough to withstand whatever outside forces push on you.

As for your internal compass, your beliefs lead you to what you do. So, if you believe that you won't land the job, that the world is against you, or you'll never catch a break, you probably won't catch one! One of my favorite little quotes comes from Henry Ford, who with his quick wit, says,

> *"If you think you can or you can't, you're right."*

To develop the mental toughness to move forward under pressure, **we must change how we react to pressure by changing how we view ourselves.** What we'll define in the chapters ahead is how to probe yourself appropriately so you finally realize how you view the world and yourself. Then, after your self-discovery, you take the necessary steps to address how you think. As the wise Napoleon Hill once said, *"The only limitation is that which one sets up in one's own mind."*

**Perspective**

Perception mainly attacks the present, but perspective is the position with which we view our future. Where are we at in life right now? How much responsibility do we have? Based on what we're doing now, are we building a bright future for ourselves? Your perspective is an essential aspect of how you view and interact with the world around you. If your perspective on life is bleak, you'll ultimately find your future looking bleak. You may have heard these sayings many times before, but after reading this book, you'll leave with a clear idea of how to make the change and be mentally tough!

Many of us don't quite know how we should view our future or our world. To understand this, you need to know how *people we admire* see the world. Did you notice I said, "people we admire?" One of the core principles of this book is to surround yourself with people who will lift you up rather than tear you down. You can't gain a great perspective of your future when your peers only talk in circles, speak negatively, and even brag about their laziness. Make a list of your friends and loved ones and honestly assess them. Are they the best people to do life with?

Once you've found your respected individuals to admire, **"we need to seek to understand first, then be understood."** This is one of the core lessons from Stephen Covey's classic book, *7 Habits of Highly Effective People*. How can we expect others to be empathetic with our worries, to help us on our way forward when we won't take the time or effort to understand where they are coming from? "Do unto others as you would have them do unto you," right? Understanding other people's views on life, from where they are positioned, helps give you more clarity on how you should view the world.

### Progression

This is my favorite of the 5 P's because I believe it is the secret to success, the secret to obtaining anything you want in life. Progressing is the **move forward mindset**, a growth mindset that always needs to improve.

Progressing is the advancement or development toward a better, more complete outcome. While everyone agrees that it's good to continually progress, most people let a small failure derail their success. Once the roads get a little icy, many people can't get past the setback. This is why you'll find in Inc. Magazine that they report most New Years' Resolutions are abandoned by January 19th. Only 19 days of effort? How do you expect to make any real momentum!?

I know it's easy to say, "just move forward," but actually doing it takes hard work and determination. I have started my life over several times and know from experience that **the only way to get to that endgame is to keep your eye on the target and keep progressing.** What's the passion, and how do I get to it? How do I stay with it? How can I do my darndest to keep the passion alive and healthy? Keep moving forward!

Throughout this book, I hope to communicate plenty of testimonials and stories about how many people have flourished in life. Not only how they prospered, but how they perished too! Through these stories, I share very practical lessons, philosophies, and habits to enact in your own life. That way, you won't have to wait 40 years to find and keep your passion.

**Perseverance**

Don't quit. Mental toughness is the ability to **move forward under pressure**. Perseverance is the steadfastness in doing something despite difficulty or delay in achieving success. While progressing is the tracking of our continually improved state, perseverance is really the clutch trait to help us deliver whenever the going gets tough.

How do you develop perseverance? You must learn how to overcome obstacles and adversity. You must develop the ability to go over, under, around, or through those things that get in the way. You will only do this if you have a master plan, a target that you're shooting for. You have unwavering, often irrational confidence that you will reach this target someday, no matter how far away that someday is! The never-quit attitude is a mindset that says, "I will continue in a forward motion towards my dreams and let nothing stop me along the way. Even if I have setbacks, betrayals, and even Mother Nature up against me, I will never lose sight of the final goal!"

You'll find that people from all walks of life, who reached their perception of what a "good life" looks like, had perseverance. While progressing is the secret sauce for improving your life, perseverance is the requirement for any mental toughness.

Ladies and gentlemen, I'm excited for you to read this! It's 40 years in the making, and it's finally time for you to build the life you've always wanted. Keep reading, underline good phrases, write notes, and start implementing these proven principles to live a great life. Let's keep moving forward!

## CHAPTER 2
# LET'S TALK ABOUT GOALS

*"What you get by achieving your goals is not as important as what you become by achieving your goals."* - Zig Ziglar

Zig Ziglar was a great hero of mine. His landmark book, *See You at the Top*, is in the top five books I recommend to people because it changed how I viewed my life and looked at the world. I will mention Mr. Ziglar quite often in this book, but as far as goals go, he was a huge advocate.

He started his career in sales and became a leading sales expert speaking to thousands upon thousands of sales professionals. He grew in success as a salesman and field manager for WearEver Cookware, a cooking products company based out of Ohio. As his success grew, his goals and passions for his career evolved. He started by simply wanting to gain monetary wealth since he was the youngest of a 12-kid family.

As he solidified his prowess in the sales world, he looked beyond himself and his means. He looked at the whole sales industry and saw that it was becoming infected with the same stigma we still see today, full of sleaziness and "gotcha" bait and switch pitches. He and other top sales professionals founded the American Salesmasters organization in 1963. With the success of his self-help books, he rose to immense heights in his motivational speaking. He started by improving the outlook for salespeople, which then evolved into improving the outlook of the everyday individual.

Zig would not have been able to reach these transcendent heights in his career without setting goals. **We become better people as a result of setting goals.** However, it doesn't help that so few people are bad at setting goals and accomplishing them. There are all sorts of acronyms (i.e., S.M.A.R.T. goals), best-practice steps, and "four easy moves" that people will teach you. I'm not one to get too technical with it all. By the end of this chapter, my goal is to give you the things I've learned that are important about setting goals, no matter what method you choose!

First of all, let me make this clear...

## SUCCESSFUL GOAL SETTING IS AN ESSENTIAL SKILL.

Along with my 5 P's, I also have come up with 3 Phases of Achievement: Passion, Goal Setting & Mindset. Once you've found your passion, it's easier to set goals that are actually implemented, therefore forming a mindset that leads to achievement in the long haul. You won't find an accomplished individual out there who couldn't master these three phases.

**Passion is the primary determining factor for achieving a great life, but it's irrelevant if we can't successfully set goals.** If you haven't been great about setting goals, don't worry.

We've all been there. I didn't think about setting goals for myself until I was in my mid-20s! And even then, I had to learn effective goal-setting skills through the school of hard knocks.

You barely get anything done unless you set goals. **Life without intention is a life without apparent purpose, and an intentional life is filled with goals.**

You might say, "Well, no Coach P, doesn't everything start with an idea? You can't set goals if you don't have passionate ideas." You're not wrong, but my definition of "a thing starting" is when the action actually occurs. **An idea doesn't successfully become a reality without action.** You and I both know plenty of people who have great ideas but have a terrible time getting those ideas to happen. That's because too many people today haven't a clue how to set goals successfully.

You might also say, "Well, I'm passionate about seeing trash being picked up in the ocean and for there to be better recycling methods. The Earth needs us!" That's a fantastic passion if it's really a passion. Too many people confuse "passions" and "interests." This is why passions are meaningless when there isn't tangible action. It's also directionless if there aren't goals laid out and accomplished. Passions are much bigger than interests, so we need to treat them more seriously and intentionally. If you really are passionate, what will you actually do?

Every company I started back in the day began with a goal in mind. Whether it was to do it better than my boss was doing it, provide for my family, or simply pump up my ego a little more, I always had a goal with every company I owned. For instance, I started in the sporting goods industry because my sports teams needed good equipment. I started coaching youth baseball and would eventually become head coach for a high school football team. For both these teams and many teams I came across, they needed a reliable supply of sports equipment. I started that company because I felt a need, and others felt the same. I took it upon myself to meet the demand!

That sporting goods business eventually moved toward screen printing because teams needed branded materials to promote themselves and equipment. Since they already bought my sports equipment, why not purchase screen printing from me too? I started that side of the business for added income to support the family and support a need people had. **Every venture I made happened through goal setting, and any venture you pursue will be better fulfilled by setting goals.**

Another critical factor for goal setting is a sense of curiosity. You can't have a life full of accomplished goals without a curiosity for how you could improve. If you ask some people what they want to improve about their lives, they'll be left speechless. If they were content with their lives, they'd at least say they were satisfied and happy! Unfortunately, many people haven't given themselves the time and freedom to think about what they could do to improve their lives. They just go day by day and always scratch their heads, wondering why life ain't that great.

This was likely an ego problem for me, but I always thought I could do anything better than anyone else. That got me into quite a few pickles, but the principle is good at heart. I would constantly ask myself an important question:

*"How can this be done better?"*

**This is the same question that anyone who achieves great things asks.** By asking this question, we grant ourselves the pathway to do a few things:

1. **We're continually improving.** If we really try and answer this question, we'll become improved individuals in the process. Even if we don't get the goal accomplished in our timeline, or at all (like Zig Ziglar confessed at the beginning of the chapter), we'll become much greater individuals by simply pursuing goals.
2. **We're constantly growing.** By asking this question all the time, we can't help but grow! We could have the best exam test results but still have room for improvement. We'll always grow if we're always looking to make ourselves better. Guaranteed.
3. **We're always moving past defeat.** There will be losses inflicted on us with unforeseen and unpredictable events that keep us from accomplishing goals. We'll always keep ourselves from going into a depressing rut by asking this question. What's even more fun is that our challenges cause us to be innovative and intelligent about how we do work!
4. **We're always motivating ourselves and others.** We'll always keep ourselves moving forward, but what's even cooler is that we will inspire others to move. By our friends, family, and colleagues see how we're always looking to be better, it'll challenge them to ask, "Well, wait...how can I be better?" **By improving yourself, you end up improving the world around you.**

But that's enough talk about why setting goals is a good thing. Let's talk about some of the items you'll need to know to create great goals.

## FIGURING OUT YOUR GOALS

If a few of you were asked about your goals in life or what dreams you wanted to accomplish, you could spit them off to me very quickly. That's great! Later on, we'll work on building a realistic timeline for your goals. What I would like to focus on here are a few questions about how to figure out your goals. There are plenty of you that are just having a tough time knowing what goals you want to accomplish!

Here are questions you can ask yourself to determine some goals:

1. **What do I do in my free time?** We all have at least some free time, so how do we spend that free time? We could be watching movies, browsing through our phones, playing video games, playing an instrument, hanging out with friends, or having lots of other interests and hobbies. **What consumes your time outside of work or school? What fascinates you?**
2. If this leaves you with unsatisfying answers, a better question is likely, **"How do you wish you spent your free time?"** Many of us can think about how we spend our free time and honestly admit some regret. We find that we're too lazy and aren't really putting in the effort to excel at the desired skill. In the back of everyone's mind, there's always some interest or some desire or some idea that we've had for a while. Interests you once had could be buried deep in your past. You might need

others to remind you of the goals you once were passionate about! **On some level, we all wish something was better.**

3. For the young people reading this book, are you wanting to be excellent at an athletic sport? Or are you wanting to get into owning your own business? What do you want to be when you grow up? **Feel free to dream because you are blessed with your young age!** No matter what anyone tells you about your capabilities, you are blessed with time, the most valuable commodity. **In time, you can figure out how to accomplish most anything.**
4. For the folks who aren't kids anymore (and even have a few gray hairs), **I would still challenge you to think about what you wanted to be when you grew up as a child**. Seriously! Why can't you do cool things with your life? Why should you settle for mediocre goals and fantasies? Because you aren't a kid anymore? Because your friends and family would think you are silly? So, what if you can't be the next Bon Jovi? Maybe you can be in a cover band and have a lot of fun playing anthems from the 80s? **Your big dreams don't have to die, even if they don't look all that big.**
5. **What did you enjoy when you were a kid?** Other similar questions include, "What did you want to be when you grew up?" or "What really excited you about the future when you were a kid?"
6. If you go back to when you were a young child, under ten years old, you'll discover that you would likely still enjoy the same things as an adult. Most adults are embarrassed to jump back into childhood pleasures, but these childhood fascinations often get lost in adulthood because it's not "realistic" to do. **Adulthood**

**squashes many childhood dreams under the disguise of "wisdom."** In reality, adults are telling you about how something isn't possible because they couldn't do it. Don't let these negative adults kill your dreams and goals.

7. **What do I enjoy the most out of each day?** What do you enjoy the most out of everything you do during your day or week? That's likely a passion and a future goal. What if you ended up doing that thing you enjoy all the time? That's the ultimate goal for your work, to make it your passion. You can also ask yourself, **"What do I look forward to each day, week, month, or year?"**
8. **What puts you at peace?** Each person has activities that they do or wish they could do. What have been those activities? Vacations often fall in this category, but what do you specifically like about vacations? Is it the beaches, camping, nature, museums, or more family time? **Find out the specific things that bring you peace and joy.**

The answers to these questions above are likely what your passions are.

If you haven't come up with any ideas yet, do not fret. Many times, it takes continual attempts at asking yourself the same questions in order to finally get any clarity. You may need to ask your family and friends for guidance on what you actually like! 20-somethings are often spending these years figuring out what line of work will give them a satisfactory life. Why can't you spend years figuring out what passions you'd love to have in life?

Everything starts with goal setting and if a passion is *really your passion*, you act. Even if it's challenging at times, you look past those challenges and still put in effort to grow and improve. **By testing your passions with actions, you discover what your passions truly are.**

Once you've decided what your goals or passions look like, you need to fit these goals into actionable steps. What will you literally do on a daily or weekly or monthly basis to become skilled in, for example, speaking French? What do you need to learn in order to get very good at catching slant routes in football? How many days do you have until basketball tryouts? Based on how many days are available, how many hours should you be at the gym working on your layups and free throws? **Assign when a goal needs to be completed (a deadline) and then schedule how frequently you need to do something in order to complete the goal.**

## HONOR YOUR GOALS

Here comes one of the hardest parts about goal setting, **you actually have to honor them.** Crazy, right? Some people think that because they're passionate, it'll be easy to do that activity. Then, why do you find so many adults who talk about how "back in the old days" life was so much more enjoyable? Passions are real when action is consistently behind them. By sticking to what you commit to, even when the going gets tough, you'll confirm whether something is really a passion or not.

What you may have decided is to temporarily pause your passions because there are more important things to worry about. You've got hungry kids that need food, unexpected bills to pay and a job that doesn't pay you enough. It's perfectly fine and normal to pause on a goal, as long as you're working toward restarting and finally accomplishing it.

In my experience, it's not good to just sacrifice and settle for a less-than lifestyle. You'll never be happy if you always think life could've been better. That's why you'll find washed up, middle-aged people who are absolutely bitter. They are good people, but they gave up on their potential too early and never became truly satisfied with life. Their passion didn't work like it was supposed to, and they ultimately settled for a life that was "just okay."

To be honest, your passions won't always be enjoyable. There are days whenever I leave the football field and the team is a mess! When players don't show up for practice, don't have the proper equipment, and aren't doing well enough in school to play football, the mental anxiety can really take a toll on you. Oh, and don't forget all the fundraising work you have to do as a coach! That's one of the hidden parts of the occupation no one knows about. After a long day, anyone could decide to give up.

But the keyword is *"could."* After those thoughts of defeat and frustration, **I take a deep breath and remember how thankful I am to have a job that provides me a great, fulfilling purpose to life.** I remind myself about how I'm glad to not be selling sporting goods anymore for a sporting goods store. I'm reminded that I can actually support my family through my passion. That's a supreme blessing.

## WRITE DOWN ANYTHING AND EVERYTHING

I'm a huge believer in writing down everything and by the end of this book, you'll be tired of me hammering this point. What do I mean by this? **Any interesting thoughts that pop into my head, I write it down.** A new blocking formation that can be good for my defensive linemen? I will write it down. A nice quote by an established business leader or writer? I will write it down. A list of groceries to pick up? I will write that down too! **If it's important to remember, it should be written down.**

I've been journaling for over twenty years now and this has been a major part of my life. I've now got bookshelves of all these different journals. While my penmanship isn't the greatest, I'll actually go back on January 1st every year and read through my old writings. When you're able to revisit your past writings, it does a few powerful things.

**It reminds you about where you came from.** Man, I have so many memories stashed in those journals and notes. It keeps me humble and shows me really how much I've grown over the past several years of my life. Even now as a mid-60's guy, I still find myself grateful and looking to improve!

My podcast and the self-improvement courses I offer (www.inspiringthem.com) are all ideas that came from my journal of thoughts I had in the past. Probably the biggest thing I do with my journals daily is to **write down negative thoughts I have throughout the day and rephrase them into a positive statement.** I then reread that positive statement four or five times throughout the day to keep my mind in a positive attitude. **I'm essentially rewiring my brain to be positive instead of negative.**

**Journaling also helps me think clearly.** When you have so many thoughts bouncing around in your head, ranging from daily jokes to life revelations, those important "life revelations" end up slipping through the cracks. Important thoughts are lost every day and that's a shame because really, you never know when an idea of yours is the next big one.

Through journaling, I was able to discover that I really had a passion for teaching and becoming a head football coach. It also motivated me to get my degree and provide online courses for motivation and life improvement! Without journaling, I'd be a man with many ideas and nothing to show for it.

How can you start journaling? Well, let's start by assuming that **most people you know don't journal and will think it's weird.** I guarantee you if you're the only one in your high school writing down things in a journal, you'll be made fun of. We can fast forward through time to your office job you've been working at for more than a decade. Now you suddenly start journaling about your life? You'll still get raised eyebrows from 40 and 50-year-olds who never decided to journal. Doing anything proactive will be a little weird to most people, but here's a life tip, **it's usually the stuff no one is willing to do that actually works.**

For me, I have bought enough journals where there's a journal pretty much anywhere I go. In the car, on the coffee table of my favorite chair, at my home office desk, at my school desk and anywhere else I might find myself; you'll find a journal! I often carry around a little note pad anyway. I really don't have to think about scheduling "journaling time."

For you fancy young people, you can also just jump on a Notes app on your smartphone and create notes that way. I guess one thing that will help you make sure it happens every day is by setting a reminder on your phone to ask, "Have you journaled yet?" **You want to at least journal something every day.** You can also do dedicated journaling times where you are thinking of nothing else except how your week has gone and what the next week looks like. The best business owners in the world write a plan for how their day should look, every day.

Here's some good questions to ask yourself while journaling:

1. How did my day go today? Or yesterday?
2. Are there things that could've been better?
3. Any funny things or interesting things I was taught?
4. What do I need to prepare for this week? Or in the near future?
5. Is there anything stressing me out?
6. How are other people I care about doing?

## DISCOVER WHAT YOUR TRUE PASSIONS ARE

Understanding your true passions and goals in life comes with great humility. We won't get everything done that we set our sights on. With time, you'll find that many of the goals you set won't be fulfilled, because you didn't actually care about them. It's not a good thing to fail at your goals, but it's better to find out what you won't care about quickly.

Over time, you'll figure out what you *really* want from life. You'll find this out only by taking action toward your passions and discovering that you don't actually like or care about whatever it is.

Growing up, I thought starting and growing super successful businesses would be my passion. As I gained multiple opportunities to start and grow companies, I discovered that I didn't enjoy the day-to-day operations. I liked creating things, but I didn't enjoy the rigor of doing the same, monotonous things over and over again. It could very well be because I didn't find the right business! Through the process though, I found out that my biggest passion was in helping people succeed, through mentorship. This led me to transition to teaching and coaching sports as a full-time career! I wouldn't have learned this if I never set goals.

**When you're getting up in the morning and looking forward to doing what you do for work or life, you've found your passions.** Until this happens, you are simply working in a job. That's it.

Temporarily, you'll need to just work a job, but I would hope that one day, you transition your life to fully working and thriving in a career that's your true passion, where you work toward your true goals. That's what I've been able to do, but it took me decades to get there. It's about time you figured it out and started now! Start setting goals and discovering your passions! You won't regret it.

# CHAPTER 3
# WHAT TO DO WHEN YOU WANT TO DO SO MUCH

Kathy Caprino, a senior contributor for Forbes, put together a basic list of ten things everyone wants in life, but in her words, "...just can't figure out how to get." Here's her list:

1. Happiness
2. Money
3. Freedom
4. Peace
5. Joy
6. Balance
7. Fulfillment
8. Confidence
9. Stability
10. Passion

This looks like any list you would create for desires in life. Who doesn't want all these great qualities? Happiness, money, and joy? Come on! These are all great things. I'm not sure why she lists "Passion" as the 10th option because, in my mind, discovering and fulfilling your passions will cause you to have all these other qualities. You are the happiest when you're in the midst of your passion. Having the financial freedom and time freedom to spend time on your passions makes it even better. You find peace, joy, and all the other traits through your passion.

What was the biggest issue that came up about why people couldn't find happiness in their lives? **They didn't know what they wanted to do.** After reading the last chapter about goals, many of you are still left a little speechless. You might be saying to yourself, *"Thanks for the material, Coach P, but I'm still a little undecided about what I want."*

Some of you have lots of ideas and dreams about what you want, but usually, when people have lots of options ahead of them, they can tend to get indecisive, for risk of picking "the wrong pathway." They could also try and do everything at once, which causes them to be average at lots of things and never truly succeed at anything. That's a lesson I'm still trying to learn! Speaking of lessons, let's review what the 3-Phases of Achievement are again.

3-Phases of Achievement: Passion, Goal-Setting & Mindset

**Once you find your passion, everything else becomes more apparent.** Whether you have lots of goals or no goals, you start by figuring out one thing, in particular, you're naturally passionate about. Or at least you find something you WANT to be passionate about. Oh, that's an important point!

**For those of us who aren't very passionate or enthusiastic people, we can catch ourselves emotionally drifting.** What do I mean? If there's a natural tendency to drift towards being lazy, we'll sail to this emotional choice. If you'd naturally like to binge-watch a tv show instead of going on a run, you'll probably watch Netflix. For these folks, it's essential to **simply decide what you want to be passionate about.** Since it's not a natural tendency, they must take what's in front of them and determine what they want to be good at.

There's a very smart book titled, *Pathetically Apathetic* that really speaks to this crowd. The author, Harley Liechty, shared how he dealt with this dilemma. He grew up financially well and had all the options in the world, but he had never built any discipline or decisiveness in his life. So, after graduating college, he found himself depressed because he was on his own and had no idea what he wanted. He had a job and a place to live but no direction or significant relationships. He asked himself, *"What am I even living for?"*

Many of you are asking this very question. You've been asking this question since before high school! When I started working for myself, I asked myself these same questions, and it took me too long to figure out any of my passions. That's why I wrote this book, and that's why you're reading it!

## START WHERE YOU ARE

In 1972, I started as a dishwasher in an Italian restaurant. A typical high school job for sure! And for any high schooler, this obviously isn't the dream job. Who wants to be a dishwasher all their lives? I'm not the type that's short on dreaming up ideas either. I have had big dreams and goals for my future since I was a young kid. So there's no way I wanted to slave through this job for long. To grow past dishwashing, I needed to learn an important lesson.

**Stay long enough to learn and achieve, then quickly leave.**

In this dishwashing job, my first lesson was discipline and working hard. I learned how to stay at one tedious task and continually do the task until it's completed. This is such an important skill to develop in work and any life pursuit. You will find ruts even in your passions where the fire isn't there. If you want to be an author, you'll find plenty of times when you don't have any good ideas to add to the book. If you are learning an instrument, you will reach a spot where you're pretty good, but getting advanced requires lots of repetition and practice; that's aggravating. If you want to dominate in real estate, you'll have to be patient in the first five years. It's a grind for sure!

I see this all the time with my football athletes. These kids have a natural talent and athleticism but constantly complain about sprints or running hills. They whine about tackling drills, even when it's been the 275th time they tackled the same dummy. They say to me, *"I already know how to tackle! Why are we still doing this?"*

**There's always a rhyme or reason for going through these repetitive tasks.** I don't want my athletes to be "pretty good" at tackling. I want them to master tackling. I want them to increase the force they exert with each tackle each day and week. I want them to still be able to tackle while they are off balance effectively. I want them to adjust within milliseconds to movements from the offense and still tackle or swat the football for a fumble. I want them to apply obliterating force on the offense, even when two minutes are left in the fourth quarter and they are drained.

Wherever you are in life, are you thriving? Are you delivering great results? Are you the best person you can be with whatever opportunities you have available? **You could already be in the best spot to find your passions and create a great life.** I like to say that ***"your current job is your greatest job."*** You create more opportunities by thinking that your current job is a great job. It motivates you to be better than average at work. People will like working with you more, and your boss will favorably recommend you.

That's what happened to me. I did an excellent job in dishwashing and then quickly moved to be a grocery store clerk, where I earned twice as much as I made in the little Italian restaurant. Since I treated the first job as the best, I attained the skills needed to be a good grocery store clerk. Those skills continually improved so that I could do even greater things, like find my wife. I would soon work better-paying clerk jobs with benefits, and within five years after my first job, I tripled my hourly wage. Sure, it went from $3/hour (dishwashing) to $10/hour (laboratory work), but $10 in 1977 equals $44/hour in today's money! That's quite the increase in earnings!

**So for deciding where to start, start by doing a great job where you're at.**

## USE MASLOW'S HIERARCHY OF NEEDS

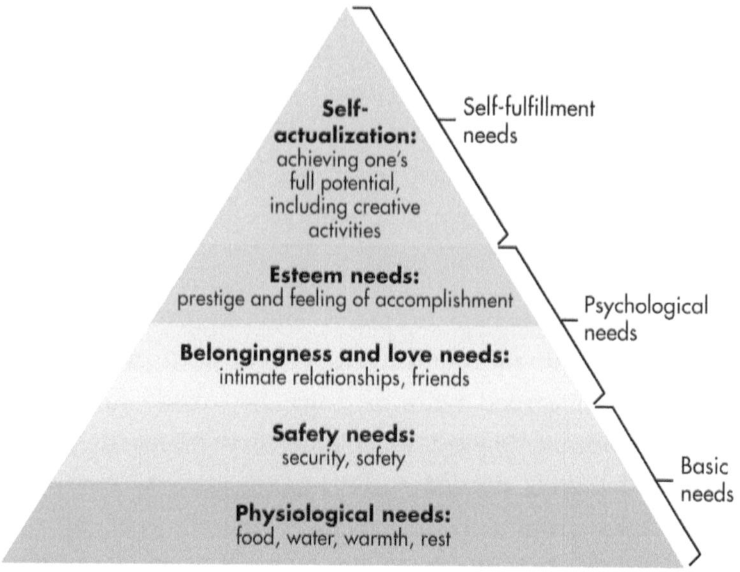


Abraham Maslow, back in 1943, released a psychology paper titled "A Theory of Human Motivation," which is where his most remarkable work comes from, his hierarchy of needs. This is a classic structure used by psychologists and thinkers worldwide to help determine what motivations need to be met first and foremost. If used correctly, the framework can be tailored to any situation to find our most significant priorities at the moment. For example, while you may want to be a surgeon, you must also put food on the table and ensure your family is safe.

Let's use Harley's development that he describes in *Pathetically Apathetic* as an example. He had a job and a place to live, so his Physiological needs were met. He didn't say anything about living in a bad neighborhood, so we'll assume his Safety needs are met. In his depression, he expressed great loneliness working from home all day, alone, with few friends to lean on. So he needs Belongingness, and he also needs to build Esteem needs since he didn't care about his work at all.

Naturally, through Maslow's Hierarchy of Needs, finding a new job with motivating people and greater fulfillment makes sense. That's precisely what he did. He had a friend from his old college who worked at a business consulting firm that offered him an opportunity. So he started there and grinded his way into the company for years to eventually receive greater financial earnings. He now has a greater sense of accomplishment in his work and has moved on to his "creative activities" with Self-Actualization goals. He's developing jazz piano skills (a passion he discovered) and has already recorded two albums!

As a young high schooler, I had my Physiological and Safety needs met, but once high school was over, I couldn't settle for $3/hour. This was especially true because in the store clerk job after high school, I met the love of my life. We would get married in 1975 and then have three children in the next five years. Talk about a lack of planning!

With each additional family member in the house, the Physiological and Safety needs were threatened. The financial demands kept increasing, so I had to improve my employment positions continually. I had to, each year, continue to maintain my Physiological and Safety needs through increased income. I couldn't adequately advance to "higher needs" if bills were difficult to pay and my family's health was jeopardized.

Once I could trust myself to maintain these needs, I moved on to fields of work that I truly enjoyed - sports. Until my late 20s, I worked in jobs that didn't excite me, but sports were always my passion. I always enjoyed baseball and football as my primary sports in school, but due to the demand of high school jobs and our poorer family, I couldn't compete at a high level as a teenager. Since I proved I could care for my family, I decided to get in good physical shape. I bulked up and became so athletic that I tried out for a semi-pro football team. It seemed like a crazy dream at the time, but I made it! This brought some income to me, but more importantly, I got to actually play football on a semi-professional team. Dream fulfilled!

While this happened, I needed other athletic, flexible jobs to maintain the family's financial needs. Because of my background in sports and my recent physical fitness endeavors, I started a sporting goods business. I would sell sports equipment to teams across the Midwest region, and this satisfied a hidden passion that had yet to be fulfilled, starting up things. This was my first exposure to entrepreneurship, and it was very empowering to see an idea come to fruition in my life and make us profits! Sports satisfied the fulfillment of my Esteem goals. I also signed up to coach baseball, which awakened my passion for coaching and teaching, a love I didn't even know I had.

See, by using Maslow's Hierarchy of Needs, we can determine the best course of action, and how it flows logically toward the greatest goals and needs, the "Self-Actualization" needs. These are the greatest of all goals, as the cherry on top of your sundae. We have the flexibility, in time and finances, to pursue extra endeavors that are more so "wants."

For some of you though, this passion talk can seem a little discouraging. You may ask me, *"Coach P, this seems like a really long time. Are you telling me it took you over a decade to accomplish your Esteem and Self-Actualization goals? I want to start my own business NOW! I want to become a big-time actor NOW!"*

I know there are plenty of people on social media and YouTube who showcase their amazing lifestyles. It's almost hard to comprehend how a 24-year-old kid already has a Bentley and a mansion in Hollywood. I don't know how helpful this will be, but I'll say it anyway. **We all start somewhere.** We all have our own unique abilities, talents, skills, and character traits. We also must realize that we have unique limitations, disabilities and conflicts that get in the way. I promise you, if you keep moving forward and master Progression and Perseverance (which we'll discuss later on), it's inevitable that you will reach this dream life you imagine. By the end of this book, I hope you truly understand this.

## YOU'LL FIND YOUR PASSIONS AT SOME POINT

In Harley's early journey, he had to discover what he wanted to do. He didn't know that jazz piano was a skill he wanted to master, but he found this out by taking action. He had to think hard about his life. He determined that he would be ashamed if he never learned this skill. And after years of practice, his love for the music didn't die but breathed new life into him.

He also discovered that some plans weren't as interesting as initially thought. For instance, Harley described how he wanted to get closer to his distant family members. He made an extensive list of names, people all in their 20s to mid-30s. He thought, *"It'd be great to form relationships with these family members."*

After a couple of months, there was no action taken. As a result, Harley focused on other priorities. He could reliably do weekly phone calls with his parents and sister, but that was the extent. Instead of whining and complaining about how he's not a good family member, he realized that this was not something he was truly interested in.

**With all of our desires, we must come to terms with reality.** We must understand that not all things are necessary at the same time. For example, if you dedicated every ounce of energy to caring for your sick mother, you can't spend adequate time in an exciting, new job across the country. You must pay bills and take care of your mother until she's passed.

At times, it doesn't seem fair. Your passions won't be exercised; you only sometimes wake up and wonder what you're living for. You'll feel stuck, just waiting for something good to happen, like a big break! The fortunate thing is that even in those depressing times, you can still use it intentionally. You can leverage the skills you're learning now for future, more excellent jobs. You can sacrifice hours of sleep or social hours to practice advanced skills. You can build toward a future you want. Anyone can do this!

Then someday, sooner than you might think, you will live a life that's entirely within your passions. That right there is something that only a few people on this Earth will ever experience. Wouldn't it be worth it to reach that point finally? Or at least try?

## START NOW, AND IT WILL ALL COME TO PASS

The biggest takeaway I can give you regarding your many hopes and dreams in life is that if you start to excel where you are, **it's inevitable that you will accomplish your desires in life.** You will find yourself in fantastic places if you always pursue growth and improvement. That's what happened to Steve Harvey.

Steve Harvey is one of my favorite comedians. If you read just a little bit about his journey, it's pretty remarkable. He was a man, like myself, who had many ideas and aspirations. From the looks of it, he tried out new things constantly but didn't see fruits in them initially. He was apparently a boxer, autoworker, insurance salesman, carpet cleaner, and mailman during his 20s. Jumping from field to field, he finally found his passion for comedy in his late 20s. He began doing standup comedy gigs at 28, and since he discovered his passion, he was hell-bent on making it work. So much so that his Physiological and Safety needs were not a concern for him. He supposedly slept in his car for three years and would shower at gas stations. Three years! That's three winters of blisteringly cold temperatures in Cleveland, Ohio!

Steve Harvey discovered his passion and pursued that love like nothing else mattered, and you could relate! If you're in high school sports right now, you could have dreams of playing in the big leagues or even for a D1 college. What does it look like to be the best athlete? You need to train harder than anyone else at your school. It would be best if you didn't stay up late every night playing video games because you need to wake up early and work out. Build up that football physique! You should also find a way to invest in supplements and dieting so you can get the most out of your body. You'll also likely need private training to get that extra assistance to the next level.

But what if these things aren't available to you? What if they are too difficult to attain? All the questions swirling around your head boil down to a single question: **Is it worth it?** And really, the only person that can answer that question is you.

For Steve Harvey, he believed that standup comedy was so worth it, he was willing to be homeless and survive with the most minimal needs possible. Doing this gave him the time needed to get better and better at comedy, to the point where he could fund greater financial necessities (like living in an apartment). Since he was so laser-focused, he began to get acclaim for his humor, to the point where tv shows and movies started calling for him. After a dozen years in standup comedy, he joined the Kings of Comedy tour, which became the highest-grossing comedy tour ever, earning $18 million and $19 million in both its tour years.

So even for Steve Harvey, it took a dozen years to reach the meteoric fame everyone dreams of. And now, we know Harvey as a television host and big-time celebrity. He's become a household name and comedy legend. Being like Steve Harvey takes this all-out commitment to one thing, where nothing else matters except achieving that dream. His whole life mindset can be summed up into one quote:

> *"If you want to be successful, you have to jump. There's no way around it. If you're safe, you'll never soar."* - Steve Harvey

Does this journey seem daunting? Absolutely, and it should! In fact, if your goals and dreams don't look a little frightening, you're not dreaming big enough.

There's something else that's important to mention. With all these goals and aspirations you have, if they aren't genuine passions (not even one of them), you won't make it. The love, the burning fire behind you to move your butt, will sustain you. Without the intense fire to achieve your dreams, you will give up. It's inevitable.

In my journey, I started pursuing my sports passions *after* a dozen years of work. Steve Harvey took a more aggressive approach and began his pursuit much earlier, sacrificing basic necessities and comforts in life. We saw Harley Liechty wrestle with what he needed to accomplish and then move toward his Self-Actualization needs. He's only been down the road for three years, but because of his burning desire to reach his goals, he's got a bright future ahead.

If you start now with a desire and passion for growing, you will accomplish goals you never even dreamed of. Do you think Steve Harvey thought about hosting his own game show (Family Feud) while trying to get paid something for standup? Of course not! He just wanted to live in an apartment instead of a car! As we can all see, his work and dedication paid off. Do you know what the exciting part is too? If you do the same things Harley, Steve Harvey, and I did, it will inevitably pay off in your favor.

Will it pay off exactly the way you envisioned it? Probably not. The Steve Harvey success stories are pretty unbelievable. And if you ask any accomplished person about their lives, they will tell you it's much better than they ever could have imagined. No matter the result, the decades and decades of dedication will be enough for you to say, "Wow, what a life I've lived." That's really what everyone wants. It's like the quote we referenced in the last chapter!

> *"What you get by achieving your goals is not as important as what you become by achieving your goals."* - Zig Ziglar

Even though I would have loved to coach in bigger leagues and continued to own businesses, I am still content and happy. Why? Well, I look back at how my life has been and can't help but be thankful. After almost 70 years, I still have my life, and many loved ones I know don't. Age does that to you. It can make you thankful, or it can make you resentful. That's your choice.

Passion is what drives these endeavors forward. There's a gut desire and itch that's so pivotal to our success. We can look at a hierarchy of needs by Abraham Maslow for inspiration, or we can look at Steve Harvey, who was hell-bent on one thing. **There must be a passion driving you!** Or else, you'll find that life can be pretty aimless. Then you'll wake up at 45 years old and wonder, "So, what am I even living for?"

**If you're stuck on where to start, just start where you're at.** What's happening right now in your life? Are you providing great value for what you do? In the illustration by Maslow, what needs are not being met? What can be done right now to solve these problems? If accomplishing these higher needs isn't possible, what can you do today to achieve these needs in the future?

Anyone who considers their life "a success" understands that this is a journey of continual pursuit. The weak give up on their dreams and live mediocre life. The strong-willed find back alleys and corners, never stopping the pursuit of their passions. When you have so much you can do, just start, and your true passions will come to fruition.

# CHAPTER 4
# THE LABELS OF THE WORLD CANNOT CRIPPLE YOU

Have you ever watched the movie, *Miracle*? Some of you kids weren't even born when this movie came out, but in 2004, Hollywood put together a film to commemorate one of the best moments in American sports history. I was fortunate enough to see this live.

In 1980, I was only in my 20s and had already started a family of three kids with my high school sweetheart. So raising very young kids and working my job was pretty much my entire life! I had yet to awaken my sports career, but there was a moment in sports that struck a chord with me. It was in the 1980 Winter Olympics, and the United States was making history, surpassing all the odds, and was headed for a showdown with the USSR. The US team was creating an ultimate Cinderella story to win the Gold medal at the Olympics.

At the time, the USSR was a dominant force of nature. Do you know how Alabama has been the absolute juggernaut team in college football, winning six national championships in a decade? Well, the USSR was even more dominant in hockey. They hadn't lost an Olympic hockey game since 1968. For three straight Olympics, they were invincible. During this time, the

United States was engaged in the Cold War with the Soviets, where anything and everything was a competition with the USSR. This is the same time as the Space Race (the race to land on the moon first) and the Berlin Blockade. For the unfamiliar, younger folks, this was when the Soviets blocked supply transportations to West Berlin and inspired over 300 days of supply airlifts to the people of Western Berlin from the United States. The competition between the United States and the USSR was fierce, but nobody saw a chance for the US hockey team to win.

If you watch the movie, they do a great job of detailing the stakes. These are just US college athletes, many of whom never turned professional! They face professionally-bred USSR hockey players who have trained their whole lives, for one thing, kicking ass in hockey. The US team had won gold back in the 1960 Winter Olympics, but they had never faced such a dominant team as the USSR. Everyone in the media questioned every player and coach on that US team. There were plenty of skeptics, and nobody thought they could become Olympic gold medal athletes.

I'll let you watch the movie for yourself, but their journey is a great lesson for one of the 5 P's necessary to practice Mental Toughness. To live a mentally tough life, you must have a positive perception of the world around you. In a relentless, seemingly crazy fashion, you must never waver. Those who are mentally tough keep the haters out of their minds and focus on the positive possibilities. In the same way, the US hockey team surpassed all the haters and worked relentlessly to prove themselves worthy of gold; we must persevere through all the warfare in our minds. **The way you perceive yourself is the way you will live your life.**

## WHERE PERCEPTION BEGINS

Perception is the image that you have for yourself. All of your thoughts, dreams, and actions you think in life are based on how you view yourself. When we're children, though, we don't understand the word "perception." There aren't many human emotions we understand as children. Children aren't born understanding why they experience "worry," "embarrassment," or "self-perception." We don't even have these emotions!

When we're at a very young age (younger than ten years old), all we're focused on is how to have the most fun life possible, all the time. It's fantastic for me to watch children play around and operate in the world. This is one of the biggest reasons why being a parent is worth it. Kids help you live an enjoyable, silly life again. There isn't a care in the world for what people think about them!

As we grow up, we experience personal revelations about the world, and all of these moments are wrapped around one central idea: **We are all influenced by how people perceive each other.** We often see this first in the classroom or playground. Whenever we get in the playground football game, it stings. Kids cry, but they don't know why yet. Then, jokes will be made if they don't wear great clothes in the classroom. We have lovin' feelings and butterflies for someone in our class but suddenly fear rejection or failure, seemingly for no reason.

There is a clear reason. We are all influenced by how people perceive each other. We watch television shows and discover new interpretations of the world; ones we would have never imagined were "important." Eventually, in everyone's development through childhood, teenage years, and adulthood,

**perception becomes what we've allowed people to label us as.** We didn't start this way, but as time passed, we were labeled and stereotyped by flaws and commonalities.

Our self-perception is easily formed by the friends, family members, classmates, and colleagues in our lives. An excellent example is when children are asked what they want to be when they grow up. If you ask most children this question, they will provide you with a profession that's ambitious or admirable. They may want to be doctors, firefighters, police officers, scientists, astronauts, or other knowledgeable professionals. As adults, we love this and encourage them to pursue greatness!

At a certain age, likely once we become a teenager, we receive labels from people. Many of these labels aren't wrong, but these labels often **define our potential.** If you are labeled as a "black kid," you suddenly get wrapped into stereotypes that encourage you to believe that you will be taken advantage of or that life will be more challenging. If you are labeled as a "nerd or geek," you are suddenly shoved into a category in school where you can't participate in sports or can't be proud of your engineering expertise.

Most of these labels are just generalizations. I mentioned earlier the label of being a "black kid." There's a gigantic history of black slavery and oppression in this country. We also have discrimination toward historically impoverished communities, with rampant crime, drugs, and gangs in this deep history. Being a "black kid" unfortunately carries a great weight for all black children to bear.

Should this mean that as a "black kid," you should automatically believe the negative stereotypes? Yes, there are real facts that can't be ignored, but should this mean you are "more susceptible" to the stereotypes just because of your skin color? Should this automatically be the perception of yourself? I say no. I say that whether you're black, white, or Asian, you can have the self-perception of a champion. You can think of yourself as the mentally tough individual you want to be! You can consider what has happened in your past and the poor behavior of those around you to say, "I will become something greater."

Too many young teenagers and children get roped into these preconceived, historical stereotypes about who they are. Even if you are labeled positively, for instance, the "top in your class," there are expectations placed on you that you didn't ask for! As a result of being labeled the "top of your class," you likely have constant pressure from your parents and other authority figures to stay focused on your studies. Because of this pressure you didn't ask for or want, you now have anxiety and worry about whether you'll "really make your parents happy." Suddenly, you've built your self-worth on your accomplishments and praise from your peers.

**The first mistake in self-perception is when you cause your labels to define who you are.** As I mentioned, some (in fact, most) labels are true. If you are only 5 feet tall and most of your other classmates are above 5 feet, then yes, you are a short kid. If you are labeled as "Asian," that's because your ancestors are descendants of Asia-Pacific countries. Many labels are accurate, but that doesn't mean it has to define who you are. But as we all grow up, we let the various labels, stereotypes, and categories, said to us by others hinder us from creating our unique identity. **If we believe these labels to be entirely true, we keep ourselves from being truly remarkable.**

It's not remarkable that you might be a "nerd," and you enjoy in-depth storyline board games. What's remarkable is how you are still a nerd and also a key player on your school's basketball team. As an adult, being labeled as a workaholic is not remarkable. What's remarkable is whenever you do work your butt off, but you also have an awesome relationship with your wife and children. Labels pigeonhole us into one category or skill, and if we aren't careful, they will define us. It can keep us from being multifaceted, remarkable individuals.

I see many kids in my school, and it is unfortunate how the bullying and labeling absolutely cripple them. Those who are smaller, not as athletic, and not as "cool" (whatever that means) feel the incessant ridicule and end up hating their time in school. They resent their peers, too, not wanting anything to do with them. In even worse situations, I believe that's why we find the massive number of school shootings. It's not the only reason, but if our children at least knew that their identity and value were not simply with the opinions of their peers in school, we'd have much fewer problems.

**The second mistake in self-perception? We never define for ourselves who we are.** I can't tell you how often I hear people say that they "aren't good at math." But really, how did that idea get into your head? Did you let other people tell you this? Did you see your grades in school and tell yourself that you aren't good at math?

What I've noticed is that people give up too quickly. We see some flaws in ourselves, and because math or science or talking to the opposite sex doesn't come easy, we label ourselves as "bad at math" or "bad at talking to girls" or "unattractive." Now, we never have any hope of being good at it!

Here's how you improve this situation: **even if everyone tells you that you aren't good at math, you don't have to submit to their judgments.** Wouldn't it be better if you committed to working hard to improve your math skills and then, after years of work, become one of the best at solving math problems? Sure it didn't come naturally, but nobody is ever genuinely great without working hard. Math is just one example. You could've been told the lie that you were a failure at presentations or fashion or being funny or at making money as an adult. **These lies likely came because one person told you that you weren't good enough! Just one idiot threw you off!**

Whatever it is, let me be the first to say that you've been lied to! You really can be great at whatever you'd like to be if you believe it to be possible. If you have always dreamed about being a great pilot in the Air Force, getting really good at golf, or building up a great financial future for your family, it's there for the taking! As I mentioned in the first mistake, you must define what you want and ignore the judgments, stereotypes, and labels placed on you by the world. **The world can't hold you down whenever you are confident in whom you need to be.**

The third mistake of self-perception is the worst one. Even when we have the talents and natural abilities to succeed at something, **we let fear and anxiety keep us from pursuing the dream.** Even if you are tall enough to make the basketball team, talented enough to learn an instrument, or intelligent enough to advance to the career of your dreams, **your perception of yourself ultimately determines whom you will become.**

This almost brings tears to my eyes. As you know, I work with teenagers all the time on sports teams and in classrooms. I overhear these conversations all the time between each other, and I hear them respond to encouragement with doubt and skepticism. Somehow, these teenagers have been discouraged from the potential for greatness, and no matter how frequently I tell them otherwise, they still carry this weight of self-doubt and fear. It's a self-perception that they wouldn't ever be good enough.

What might be even more sorrowful is that I see this all around me in the adult world! I see my colleagues stay in the same job even if it's miserable. I see friends getting divorced from their spouses or staying in a marriage that harms their health. I see other friends, who are overweight and losing hair, beat themselves up all the time because of their physical appearance. These perceptions we have of each other are killing us! **Do you realize that if we simply made a mental shift about how we think, we would be able to solve our problems and prove the haters wrong?**

How does self-doubt and fear get planted into our minds? It all starts at a young age, and then these negative thoughts grow into deep roots over time. You could've had a father who failed at accomplishing his dreams. As a result, he never taught you how to dream and confidently go after your goals. Now, you don't even know what it's like to dream big. You might have grown up in a poor family circle, and because of this, you are surrounded by people who "never have enough money." Now you believe you'll never have enough money! You could be in a racial category infected with many negative stereotypes. Because of this, now you believe "the whole world is out to get you."

Reader, let me remind you that none of these ideas came from you. All of these self-doubts, preconceived notions, and fears came from everyone around you. If there's one lesson you need to underline, highlight, and remember from this chapter, it's that **your perception of who you are is ultimately determined by you.**

## HOW TO COMBAT THE WORLD'S LABELS

**First of all, we need to define for ourselves whom we want to become.** Any personal change only comes by being honest with whom we want to be. Are you tired of never understanding how to solve your financial problems or math problems? Well, why don't you spend some time studying how to be better!? I'm sure in no time, you'll become quite the whiz at crunching numbers.

**Whatever you envision for your life, write it down and define it.** Make it very clear and written in big letters. Write down who you are in multiple places around your house or apartment. Even if you aren't awesome at something like chess, just write this statement somewhere: "I Am Great at Chess." This could sound silly, but trust me. You aren't lying to yourself. **The lie you were told is that you could never be good at chess because your parents were never good at chess or you didn't have "good grades."**

Repeat to yourself every day who you are, as ridiculous as it may seem. Over time and much hard work, you will become that person. This idea is almost a century old; when Napoleon Hill talked about it in his famous book, *Think and Grow Rich.*

> *"If you think you'll lose, you're lost. For out of the world we find, success begins with a fellow's will-It's all in the state of mind. If you think you are outclassed, you are. You've got to think high to rise. You've got to be sure of yourself before you can ever win a prize. Life's battles don't always go to the stronger or faster man, but sooner or later, the man who wins is the man WHO THINKS HE CAN!"* - Napoleon Hill

In the 3 Phases of Achievement, we have our passions figured out and understand that we need to define goals for ourselves. Mindset is that vital last part! We have no hope of being able to create a great mindset of growth until we believe that we can. If we tell ourselves that we really are worthy of being great, then we will be! It's that simple!

This is where another great combatant to the world's labels comes in: **we must give ourselves great "self-talk."** This is your internal dialogue, conscience, or Jiminy Cricket from Pinnochio! Man, some of you kids don't even know who Pinnochio is, which is an awful shame.

When it comes to perception, we need to have an internal voice to communicate great encouragement and motivation. There are many resources out there for attaining excellent self-talk practices.

Let's boil self-talk down to just three basic principles.

**Healthy Self-Talk Starts With Thankfulness**

Thankfulness heals plenty of awful circumstances. Whenever you give yourself a moment to pause and get out of a negative funk, remind yourself of why you should be thankful. It can be a challenge, believe me! It no longer becomes a challenge when you consider the possible issues of others around you.

Living in the United States makes your chances of recovery and success astronomically better than in most countries. You aren't dead yet, and on top of that, you're probably relatively healthy. Even if you're not in the best physical condition, you have reliable medical care available, most of which is covered by insurance. This is a luxury.

You can even be thankful for the negative things in your life. Why? Because you had negative moments that you surpassed in your life, right? You're not dead, and that's worth some praise. People ask me when I'll have a bad day, and I'll respond, "Well, I'll definitely have a bad day when I don't see myself in the mirror." That means I'm dead!

Through thankfulness, we can spin anything into a positive circumstance.

**Healthy Self-Talk Encourages Us to be Better Than What the World Thinks**

By giving ourselves positive self-talk, we give ourselves a great motivator. We give ourselves a challenger who only wants to see the best in ourselves. People often don't know how to communicate this way and don't have anyone in their life to be this motivation.

That's why you should listen to my daily podcast! *The Mental Toughness Podcast with Coach P* was made for people who must continually discover how to motivate themselves daily. As I said, there are plenty of other sources, but mine is pretty good!

Here's one of the testimonials from my podcast as an example of what continual, positive self-talk can do to someone! From Michael, one of my listeners - *"For the past few weeks, I discovered a gem and have been following The Mental Toughness Podcast with Coach P - Coach "P" every morning after my daily meditation. Each day is a new lesson with the adopted belief that if you have the right mindset, you can achieve anything you want in life. Seize the day and have a great weekend everyone."*

Until you become a great self-motivator through your self-talk, you'll always be a "debbie downer," believing the world is fighting against your success. No greater lie has ever been told!

**Healthy Self-Talk is Honest About the Actual Limitations We Face**

Your self-talk is also the perfect tool for communicating honesty with yourself. When you have an unrelenting cheerful voice in your life, that voice also helps give you the feedback you need. It's the kind of feedback you'll respect because it's coming from a positive source. A total jerk could give you the same advice, but because they are a jerk, you don't listen. I wouldn't listen either!

**That's the funny thing about receiving healthy, honest feedback; it must come from a positive source.** If it doesn't, it isn't respected. Whenever I owned my businesses, I noticed that employees who followed my instructions had a great relationship with me. They liked me as a human being. That's actually one of the first steps in sales. If the customer doesn't like you or your company, they will never buy from you!

This works the same way with yourself! **If you don't like yourself and who you are, there's no way you'll respect your honesty.** It's a little trippy how this works, but healthy self-talk is one of the best ways to build up a great self-perception.

So we can define ourselves and create healthy self-talk, but before we wrap up, two other things help combat the world's labels. I'm a big believer in journaling. I mentioned it before, but as you define who you want to be, you must always write it down. Journaling is your constant, positive feedback loop about who you truly think you are. By ending each journal entry positively, you will think more highly of yourself sooner than you think!

---

Finally, it's undeniable that you need good friends and family members to build yourself up. You can't create a great personal perception without the help of others. We're also social butterflies, and the reason why anyone gets to accomplish anything significant is because of good friends and family members. If you find any respected celebrity, business owner, and esteemed individual, you will find them thanking their friends and family for helping them reach their accomplishments.

Most of the time, people have good friends and family because *they* are a good friend. When you become a good friend to others, you suddenly find that people become nicer to you and considerate of your feelings. Wonder why that is? Don't you think more fondly of someone when they took time to praise your interests? Or just talk to you? It's a simple lesson but an essential reminder for all of us.

**No accomplishment or reward is valid until you think highly of yourself.** Maybe you don't think highly of yourself, and that's why you're reading this book. Perhaps the world has placed terrible labels on you and has beaten you up. These labels of the world cannot cripple you. It's time you started believing you are the person you want to be. Then not only will your self-perception be unstoppable, but your perspective on whom you will become can undeniably be great.

Let's save that for the next chapter.

# CHAPTER 5
# SEE A FUTURE THAT LOOKS GREAT

## HOW I PROVED THE HATERS WRONG

Here is a funny fact, I hated high school. Might be surprising since I'm now a high school football coach and teacher, but high school was not enjoyable for me.

Growing up, I was a real small kid and with most small kids in school, I was made fun of purely due to my size. "Short kid" or "little kid" or "not big enough" were thrown out at me incessantly. These names, insults and labels made me furious. I thought the world was against me, and everyone wanted to bring me down. This cut a huge chip on my shoulder and was a motivator to "prove the haters wrong." I would beat myself up about my physique every day, telling myself, *"They can't tell me I'm small forever. I'll show 'em!"*

Much of this insult came because I did love sports. Growing up, I loved football so much and had a dream to play on the high school team. For any small kid, this would seem like an insane thing to imagine. Attempting to tackle classmates who are 200 pounds and easily squat twice your weight doesn't seem like a great idea! Even still, this was the outlet I saw as my way to beat up on the guys who had been beating up on me.

But my athletic career in high school was slim to none. My parents told me I couldn't play football. They wanted me to play baseball instead because this was a safer sport. Even my parents judged me based on my size! This only fueled my anger even more.

Because of this, I decided to "punish my parents" and not play any sports in high school. I was actually a pretty good baseball player too, but my rebellion toward my parents kept me from seeing any other options. This actually created a split from some of my friendships I had in high school. They knew I was good at baseball, and they wanted me to play. I refused and I didn't care. **I wanted to spite the world but wasn't given an opportunity I liked.**

After the doors were closed for playing football, I just wanted to get out of high school as soon as possible. I took extra classes during the summer and finished high school a year earlier than everyone else. I then started working at the Italian restaurant, and my working career began. When I finished high school, I was 5'4" and weighed 120 pounds. A small kid indeed!

After the next couple of years, though, my family and I discovered that I had actually been growing up with an overactive thyroid. This kept me at such a small size because no matter how much food I consumed, it just wouldn't stick to my muscles and bones! My thyroid would pump the food I consume straight through my body. After working with doctors for a while, I was cured in the early twenties of my overactive thyroid. Once this occurred, my physical size shot up. I had always worked out my body, but now, I started seeing real results, which was exciting. I aggressively wanted to do it more. My opportunity to prove the haters wrong revealed itself.

I trained on my physique more and more, and by the time I was in my late twenties, I transformed into a 6′2″ man weighing 280 pounds! This was a shocking turn of events, and I was on an emotional high because of this. The petite teenager persona placed on me in high school is now way in the past. I'm a big, intimidating man now!

17-year-old Coach Jim Pusateri

27-year-old Coach Jim Pusateri

My interest in sports never died down. I still wanted to be a football player like one of my heroes, Walter Payton. Once I saw my body transform, the dream of football started to get suggested to me. It could really be possible! So, after training my butt off, I joined a semi-professional football team and played linebacker for the next 7 years. I worked as a semi-pro football player from 26 to my early 30s. The dream was fulfilled and still continues to amaze me.

---

Ever since I was young and heard all the labels placed on me by the world and my peers, I always wanted to prove the doubters wrong. I was on a mission and always needed something to strive for. This has been a theme really for my entire life, where I always need to see myself grow and take on new things. By starting businesses, finding new career skills, running political campaigns, getting college-educated, launching my podcast, and writing this book, I accomplish this goal of continuously growing and improving.

**This same attitude, of always looking to grow and advance for a better future, is precisely what a healthy perspective looks like.** My motivations weren't the greatest for fostering a better life, but we'll talk about that in a second. What needs to be understood is for **you to have a mentally tough life, you need to always see a future that looks great, no matter what happens.** Without a healthy perspective on life, you won't have any apparent reason for wanting to make your life better.

## YOU CAN SPITE OR SHED LIGHT ON THE WORLD

While I created a much better future for myself, it started from a place of inadequacy and poor self-worth. It started with loss and depression; for most people, that's the inspiration we need to improve ourselves! **Why would you improve yourself if you already believe you're the best thing since sliced bread?** The bad part about my development is that I took on the world like it was out to get me, as if life was set up as a game to make me a continual loser. This is never something I would recommend now.

Why, you might ask? **This chip on my shoulder created resentment towards people.** I grew up looking at people as "my enemies." Well, maybe it wasn't that harsh, but I felt I needed to prove myself to everyone. I grew angry at people, and my temper would flare up too frequently. I was a feisty guy and didn't have substantial control of my emotions. They didn't teach you how to stay calm and collected back in the '70s! Everything was about "freely expressing yourself," so I expressed myself with an iron fist to show the world why I really am great.

Then, once I turned 21, I could freely partake of a fond love I found, alcohol. This became a vice for me to calm down my nerves and relax. Alcoholics eventually find out that alcohol only exaggerates the natural tendencies we have. So while I believed alcohol mellowed me out, it was simply used as a distraction from my problems. It also caused me to get into too many fights and pickles with people. So while I grew up and proved the haters wrong, I also made myself look like a fool many times.

This got so bad that whenever I worked at the grocery store as a stock clerk at about 22 years old, I would work late night shifts because I would be restocking the store's aisles. I arrived at work plastered drunk and made a mess of myself on one of their aisles. One of my bosses saw plenty and promptly fired me from that job, right on the spot.

This was a very humbling experience for me, as you can imagine. I decided to no longer go on late-night drinking binges. Or at least I thought I would stop. It took me twenty more years of heavy drinking at home and too many regrettable moments to finally convince myself that the drinking needed to stop. I didn't enjoy who I was when I drank. I didn't like the resentful, argumentative, pessimistic self that came out when I was drunk.

I detail these downfalls because they were rooted in a poor perspective on life. **I believed that everyone would be out to get me as I continued to grow up and advance in my career.** Since I got picked on so much in school and the avenues to prove myself worthy were denied to me, I took matters into my own hands. I didn't trust anyone else to help me. I avenged my reputation. This left a trail of self-loathing, depression, alcoholism, and spitefulness against everyone.

My first lesson in perspective? **If you improve yourself because of what the world thinks of you, you have the wrong attitude.** I'm still a fan of proving the haters wrong, but I have different motivations now. I look at my future and see a better day than I had today. I envision a life where my grandkids and children continue to stay in touch with me. I see a future where the football team I coach does a great job, and everyone on the team develops themselves into stellar all-star athletes and people. I see a future where I'm still married to my wife, and we're getting even more in love as life continues. I see a future where I'm still looking to grow and advance in life!

**The future I see has nothing to do with the opinions of others.** That's how you've got to live life! If your motivations to improve are based on people's approval of you, well, then I'm sorry, but you'll never be satisfied. Your rosy future of everyone loving who you are will never come to fruition. Even if it does, that moment will be brief, and you'll become resentful of people who disapprove of who you are.

This adjustment in my perspective came from reading a lot of books, books from people like Zig Ziglar. If there's anything you might need right now, it's a clear focus on what future you want; what perspective you'd like to have about your life. Zig has a great quote about distractions that are so true. In his book,

*See You at the Top*, he says, "Rich people have small TVs and big libraries, and poor people have small libraries and big TVs." Books and education help give you the focus and priority you need to be a more educated, improved individual. When have televisions ever done this for people?

When you listen to the sad things of the world and associate yourself with miserable people, your view of your future will inevitably be bleak. Too many people I know don't even realize that they have lousy friends and family members. This is why I pointed out at the end of the last chapter that **you need to have trusted, positive friends and family in your life.** These people will point out who are the bad seeds in your world and give you sound advice and help when you need it most. The bad friends will bring you back down and remind you about how horrible life is.

To be honest, my friends weren't impressive in my early twenties, and many of you reading this book don't have the most incredible friends and family either. **So how do you change your perspective on your future? You read and consume positive knowledge.** You seek sources online that motivate you and encourage you to be your best. You listen to older voices like Zig Ziglar, Dale Carnegie, or Napoleon Hill. You listen to newer voices like Dr. Jordan Peterson, David Goggins, or my podcast! While the world has so much negativity, it has lots of positive influences too. You just have to seek it out like your life depends on it! So my second lesson in having a healthy perspective? **Make sure you are consuming good, positive, motivating knowledge from friends, family, and whatever else you listen to.**

Another challenging quote that Zig Ziglar gives touched me at the core. *"If you go out looking for friends, you're going to find they are very scarce. If you go out to be a friend, you'll find them everywhere."* Our culture is a very selfish one. I believe we can all agree with this, but the agreement doesn't mean things have changed. Whenever I talk with my teenagers in class about what they want to do, they always tell me, "if I just got this opportunity, then I could do it." They seem to believe they don't have the tools available to make a positive life happen for them.

Well, I got news for you. As a man in his 60s, I promise you that life will always have its limitations. There will always be excuses for why you can't do something. Friends will let you down, and you will lose close loved ones way sooner than you might want. It's easy to beg the world to give you all the desired rewards, but what are you offering in return? **Is what you contribute regularly deserving of praise and adoration?** Napoleon Hill has a stellar quote about this: *"The man who does more than he is paid for will soon be paid for more than he does."*

My third lesson on fostering a healthy perspective? **Those seeking to help others succeed will soon find themselves more successful.** There's an attraction to people who are friendly and helpful. This can be from someone your age or someone much older than you.

In my line of work, this happens every day. In the most recent football season I had, I just joined the team as the new head coach. The football team hadn't won a game in 2 ½ years, and they hired me to help them build a great football program. Quite the challenge, huh? You could peg a number of reasons for their lack of success, but do you want to know the top reason? They didn't think they could become winners.

These kids had been used to losing and couldn't imagine a world where they could be great players. When I started the first season, I had 19 seniors on my team. Only five of them finished the season. It was a rough season, with little success, but the five seniors that stuck around found something more significant than a winning season: a winning perspective on life. They learned they had the talent and the mental toughness to persevere. They knew there was greatness inside them.

This might inspire some of you to think about what you look to achieve in life. For the past few years, you could've asked yourself why the world doesn't seem to think you're all that great. In most cases, though (and in my case), it's a matter of looking at yourself in the mirror. Do you believe you're really that interesting? **If you wouldn't want to hang out and spend time with yourself, why would others want to?** Do you think that you will continue to become a more exciting person? Will you always look to help others be more successful? Can you be the friend to lift someone up when everyone else is putting them down?

That's why my original motivations for were negligible. Since I was spiteful towards my peers, my life didn't look all that great and exciting. Instead, if I looked to be the light in the world, I might have too many friends and opportunities! As Napoleon says, *"if you provide more value than what you're paid for (or what's expected of you), you'll soon receive more blessings and financial earnings."*

When I switched to no alcohol and ambitiously provided more value for those around me, I saw this happen in my life. I saw a transformation in my view of the world. The world isn't against me, but rather, the world is there for the taking!

---

See a future that looks great, a future where you're a friend to those who need you, and your decisions are based on whom you dream of being, not what others believe you are. Right here, you could take notes on what the dream, future self looks like. It's closer than you think!

## WHAT DOES YOUR FUTURE SELF LOOK LIKE?

# CHAPTER 6
# EIGHT STEPS TO A POSITIVE ATTITUDE

*"Coach P, please don't tell me to just '**think more positively.**' My problems can't be solved by just the snap of a finger and a smile!"* - A quote from one of the skeptical readers of this book

---

We're all taught from a young age to keep a positive attitude. It's common knowledge and wisdom to always "keep your cool" and never let your emotions get out of hand.

Easier said than done, folks. For the most part, everyone has a tough time with this. To be honest, I'm the same way. During just about every football game I coach, there will be moments where I yell at a player in a negative tone. The heat of the game gets to me as I'm attempting to orchestrate a great plan of action to beat the other team. My job security, annual income, and career qualifications are based on my sports teams' performance. Every game has an impact, not only on the school and the students but also on me!

Then, when my wide receiver doesn't remember the route for that specific play four times in a row, and it leads to an interception from the other team? Ugh…let's just say it's hard not to throw a table and blow a fuss! I've regretfully done this enough times to notice the pattern and calm myself down a little bit. It's not uncommon for me to throw a fit and then have to come back and apologize for my behavior.

I remember one situation where I went off on the referee for not calling the play a touchdown. It was clear to me from the sideline that the player was over the white line! I was infuriated. How could the referee be so blind? Isn't this his job? Then, I took a few more glances at the end zone during halftime and noticed the end zone lines were painted a different color (orange). I humbly walked to the referee and apologized since all my ranting and complaining were pointless, and my player was definitely on the 5-yard line instead.

This often happens with my coaching, and it continues to be one of the few things I still work on regularly. Therefore, personal evidence shows that most of us struggle to keep a cool head. The ups and downs in life make us ride quite the rollercoaster! Then you end up throwing up out the side of your chair and wonder how this fun life went wrong.

It's pretty easy to be positive when things are going great. When you get a new job, there's a giddy excitement about the potential for a better occupation. When you were responsible for helping the company reach its sales goals, it feels good to be praised and given a promotion. When you're in school and pass the science exam with an A? Wow! You didn't even know you had it in you!

In fact, I hypothesize that **most people feel the greatest whenever there are no worries about their lives.** It's pretty apparent when you think about it. People are often thrilled when they are on their honeymoon or downtown for a night out, "living their best life." Whenever you choose not to think about anything and chill out, it's very blissful. It's the easiest way to keep a positive attitude. No responsibilities? No problems!

That's why adults always want to remember when they were carefree kids. Don't you hear adults sometimes remark, "Man, I'd love just to be a little kid again?" Being an adult has hundreds of challenges that a child couldn't even comprehend! Paying rising mortgages, maintaining a loving family, constant car repairs, making sure your boss at least tolerates you, keeping your yard nice, buying gifts for people, being anxious about what the government might do or not do next...the list is endless! When adults think about being a kid again, this is why they think about it!

For the most part, adults survive through the rigors of life. Then, they take vacations to actually enjoy themselves and relieve their worries. High schoolers have these same thoughts. The new pressures of social groups, staying on top of homework, passing exams, and not embarrassing yourself publicly are unique struggles for them. So when we think back to a time with no responsibilities and a carefree attitude? It sounds nice. Unbelievable even!

But, there's a flaw in this. See, I can think back to when I was a child and reminisce about the "good 'ole days," too. I can think back to how the United States was, how we used to run around in neighborhoods freely as kids and wouldn't need to worry about "predators" on street corners. Even in poorer neighborhoods, you had adults who would watch the kids and ensure nothing wrong happened to them. We didn't have technological distractions that kept us from being outside and caused severe loneliness. If we were bored, we either developed a good work ethic or great friends.

**But if I, Coach Jim Pusateri, live in the past, then I'm living in a fantasy world.** I'm not a child anymore. I have kids and grandkids now. I have a home and an economy to worry about. I have a football team to coach and many kids to mentor, inside and out of the classroom. Other friends and family members rely on me to be there for them. **If I keep thinking back to the "good 'ole days," I can never be cheerful and happy with my current days!**

We have a terrible time keeping a good attitude because **we fail to be content with our current lives.** Social media gives us endless lives, photos, and videos "where the grass seems greener." All we see is what *they* have and what *we don't have*. We start believing that the world is totally against us and that we'll never be happy with our lives.

As a man who's seen a lot (because I've lived a long while), I can tell you that problems never stop coming. This entire book is about being mentally tough, and persevering through all of life's challenges. **Maintaining a positive attitude through it all is one of the most significant accomplishments you can ever hope to achieve.** If you can go through any trauma or trial and positively recover, you have an undeniably great life ahead of you. Before the end of this chapter, I will provide you with eight steps to become a more positive person. They are simple but blissfully effective.

## STEP 1 - JOURNALING

I'll keep talking about this until it's drilled into your skull! **Journaling is one of the most powerful ways to improve yourself.** Once a dream, plan, or vision for your life is written down, it's no longer a fantasy. It's the first step to bringing whatever you want to reality!

To your relief, journaling doesn't have to be done in one specific way. Whatever stereotype or skepticism you have about journaling "working for you" needs to be eliminated. The brightest minds in the world write down everything! The main point of journaling I want to drive home is that it gives you space and time *to think.* **Journaling gives you space and time to think, to take a deep breath, and consider your life.** This can be done in various methods.

**Diaries**

This is the way most people think of journaling. You break out your notebook and freely write about your day. This method of writing helps you process what has transpired in your day and clears up your thinking about current life events. It gives you that space and freedom to re-evaluate and ponder. It's a practice conducted by ancient greats like Leonardo da Vinci, Mark Twain, and Charles Darwin and by current celebrities like Jennifer Aniston and Oprah Winfrey. It's a critical task done by stand-up comedians worldwide to hone their craft and find great bits about life's little humorous moments.

So many people do this because we tend to make ourselves too busy. That's a consequence of America's highly praised "go-getter" mindset. We're very good at keeping ourselves busy, but we're not very good at thinking about whether our activities are really worth it. A best-selling author named John Mark Comer puts it this way,

*"The solution to an over-busy life is not more time. It's to slow down and simplify our lives around what really matters."* - (from his best-selling book, *The Ruthless Elimination of Hurry*)

Spending extended periods writing in a diary regularly forces you **to digest what happened in your day.**

**Writing To-Do Lists**

This is the proactive way to write down what happens in your day. Many people wake up each morning and just go, go, go! They run out the door with their hair on fire, from one thing to another, and at the end of the day, they don't believe they accomplished anything meaningful! When I was a business owner, this would be a frequent occurrence. Small business owners wear so many hats in their businesses. From filing taxes, paying employees, selling jobs, following up on quotes, sweeping the office floor, and everything in-between, small business owners almost run themselves to the grave!

I learned over time that if I don't proactively plan what my day needs to look like, everyone else will plan my day. And let me tell you, those are my least favorite days. You become an order taker instead of taking order of your day. Creating to-do lists and scheduling when those items will get done will help you feel like a proactive machine!

**Maintaining & Writing an Active Calendar**

And yes, if you use a to-do list, I suggest you also use a calendar. When people use to-do lists, the items on the list often pile up to multiple pages of items that "have to get done as soon as possible." If you end every day having lots of uncompleted items on your to-do list, then every day, you feel a little bit like a failure! You may even feel like it's hopeless to catch up!

**That's why you need your schedule to match what your to-do list looks like for the day.** This is so that at the end of each day, you have a chance to knock out everything on your to-do list. You would feel so accomplished! You might ask, though, "That sounds great, Coach P, but what if I just don't have enough time to get everything done?"

Then the problem isn't with your time because even Jeff Bezos has the same amount of time as you. He might work harder than you, but that's not a valid excuse either. People like Jeff Bezos get things done because of the number of things they say no to. You likely think you can't do everything because you've agreed to do too much.

This truth is tough to swallow because we feel like everything is important! Once you regularly use a calendar and a to-do list, you'll discover that there just isn't enough time for everything. **By force, you must say no to something.** If you don't, there's no way you'll keep a positive attitude! If you end up feeling like you're always trying to catch up and never get everything done, you go to bed with a negative attitude. That's never fun.

See, there are three ways right here where you can write down events and your life to give yourself time to think and consider what's best. This just scratches the surface, however. You could also use whiteboards, scrapbooks, writing partners, print calendars, dream journals, and notecards! There are so many ways for you to digest the world around you and figure out how you can uniquely become more positive and happy with life. **You've just gotta want it!**

## STEP 2- REFLECTION EACH NIGHT BEFORE BED

In my opinion, the essential part of your next day is the night before. Taking a moment to reflect on how the day went the night before helps you answer these three questions:

1. What went well today?
2. What was lousy today?
3. How will I change the bad to good tomorrow?

I prefer to do all my scheduling and planning the night before the next day. That way, you've cleared the current day out of your mind and prepared for the next day. You've put to rest today's AND tomorrow's problems.

Most people can't rest because they haven't thought about a plan to address their problems! The way most people live is reactionary. They get caught in the emotional angst of a circumstance. Because of this, they can't even calm themselves down to think through a problem. Therefore, they can't sleep well, and their next day can't be amazing because they're drowsy and stressed. By taking a moment to pause peacefully and reflect on your problems, the problems are not so big. You've given yourself space to think, and very few people do that.

## STEP 3 - WHAT'S YOUR WHY?

With anything you do in life, even if it's going to the grocery store, **you have to have a why.** With each action, even simple ones, it's good for us to understand its positive purpose. When I go to the grocery store, for example, I have my list, and I look at nothing else. My "why" is to complete the list that I created and move on to the next thing. This keeps me from wandering around the store and buying things that I don't actually need. We've all dealt with that, right? Plus, if I stray, that takes up more time than I want, which gets in the way of other things I want to do.

But then you might say, "Yeah, Coach P, I also make a list for the groceries, but I see those twinkies, and I just WANT THEM!" **Well, the only way you stick with something is by identifying why you want to do something.** You create a list for your groceries because (a) you want to stick to a budget for said groceries, and (b) you want to keep yourself healthy by NOT consuming twinkies. Oh, and (c), you set a fitness goal for keeping yourself from eating sweets this year. Now, if your goals this year included stuffing your face with as many sweets as possible, then don't stop at twinkies! Get Zebra Cakes, actual cake, and then deep-dish pizza (the cake of pizzas). You build a grocery list to keep you on track! If you don't follow it, then what good is it for?

See, this is why I love coaching. Coaching helps you learn everything from organization skills to time management, leadership, and communication. I enjoy the competition. It excites me! And while there's a love for the sport, the real why behind it is mentoring young kids to become great adults in life. **Winning and victory don't determine who we are. It's just part of what we do.** To me, there are more significant lessons learned from football than just the game. I can confidently say that every day I coach or teach in schools, I positively affect a student. That means the world to me.

If your why in life isn't that strong, you need to break out your journal and figure out your why! Why do you get up in the morning and do anything? Why does that matter? It almost sounds insane, but asking yourself why is super revealing. It helps you clearly realize the deep meanings behind your actions. It enables you to embark on the search for your purpose in life. I know you'll have to wrestle with this, but take it from me. I wrestled with this topic my whole life, and it's completely worth it.

## STEP 4 - YOUR PASSION AS YOUR CAREER

Once you determine your why, you'll have a much easier time discovering your passion (as we discussed in chapter 3). Once you discover your passion, your positive attitude comes from your pursuit of making your passion your career. I lived for many decades before I made coaching and teaching my livelihood. If you can figure out what makes you tick and what your passion is, you won't just have a "job" that you work in. You have a passion you thrive in!

Do you know how there are just those people that are always happy? They may not be the wealthiest or flashiest, but they just have a positive vibe? It's because they've made their passion their livelihood. Once this happens, you no longer have to "motivate yourself" to have a good, joyous day. Your day is positive because you're doing what you love to do!

## STEP 5 - CHANGE YOUR ENVIRONMENT

If you are always in a negative attitude, you might take a look around and listen. It could be because the people around you aren't positive. When you go to work, do you have coworkers who constantly complain and moan? When you go to school, do you have classmates that wish they were literally anywhere else except school? And all they do is complain and whine? If you notice that none of your friends are complimenting people or being positive, **you should find new people to be with.**

The problem is that some of you are forced to be where you are. This is especially true for my students in high school. It's unfortunate, but the good kids I get to talk with just have people in school that are terrible influences. The kids around them make fun of them and only degrade people. It's a shame; I get it because I was one of those kids in school.

When kids (and adults) are in a situation where they can't change the environment right now, alternative measures must be taken. **Listening to podcasts is great for keeping a positive attitude.** My podcast, the *"The Mental Toughness Podcast with Coach P,"* has been growing with more and more people sharing great feedback about how it's helped them. Here are just a couple of testimonials from the listeners:

> **Michael Tirgardoon -** *"For the past few weeks, I discovered a gem and have been following The Mental Toughness Podcast with Coach P - Coach "P" every morning after my daily meditation. Each day is a new lesson with the adopted belief that if you have the right mindset, you can achieve anything you want in life."*

> **Elsie (from the United Kingdom) -** *"Hi Coach P, just wanted to drop a thank you – I recently discovered your Mental Toughness podcasts and they have truly made such a difference in my mentality, approach and confidence in my business. All the best! Elsje – United Kingdom."*

That's what's unique about doing a daily podcast. Not only does it fuel me and give me the pep talk I need, but it's fueling others (like my friends in the United Kingdom) who need that encouragement to keep them going! **We always have the choice**

**of creating our own positive environment.** It's just that sometimes we can't choose the physical environment, so we must create our own environment with podcasts, books, and sources that aren't in our immediate circle of friends and family.

To all my high school students, let me remind you that I lived in your shoes. I was a small kid who struggled with inadequacy. The way I got through it was not healthy. I reacted by being against everyone and proving everyone wrong, which drove me too heavy drinking, resentment, and a delay in learning that teaching was my calling.

**Please, I plead with you, take small steps to seek positivity and a bright future eagerly.** Find good adults and teachers who will encourage you. Make friends with other kids who are positive and share interests or circumstances that you do. At the very least, you have each other as support. Challenge your circumstances! There's no reason why your life must be miserable.

## STEP 6 - GET OUT OF YOUR COMFORT ZONE

This might seem counter intuitive. You would think you have a positive attitude when you're comfortable with life, right? Isn't comfort part of contentment?

Let's think about this. You work hard to get yourself a house you like, someday find a spouse you love, and then make your passion your career. Once all of this happens, you can be done, right? Well, not exactly. If you get to this point and say that "you're done growing or trying to improve," you'll find some unintended, adverse events start to take place.

**After attaining great things, you must work to keep them.** You have to maintain the house. You have to foster a good relationship with your spouse continually. You need to make sure you're getting better and better at the career you're so passionate about. Although you've made it to your dream life, **you must constantly challenge and improve where you are.** The moment you stop trying to be better, you'll drift. Someone else will be promoted above you because you stopped giving 110% effort like you used to. After a long dry spell in your marriage, your spouse may be tempted to look at other mates. If your home looks like a dump, you'll start to feel like a dump! Now, you've lost what you worked so hard to initially gain.

And you know what, life happens! Some of you reading this might say to yourselves, "Yes, that's all good, but I still lost something or someone dear to my heart, even when I continually worked hard. Is this even worth it?" I remember during the recession of 2008, I lost everything. Everyone lost so much. In less than two years, I was financially back to where I was in my 20s. I had to give up my coaching position to find full time employment.

**Whether I wanted it or not, life made me leave my comfort zone.** If I shrink and give up, I wouldn't be back to coaching sports and mentoring people! I wouldn't be a college graduate! You see, it's almost like life gives us challenges we didn't ask for, knowing that if we decide to seize the challenge, we'll be more extraordinary as a result. "Woe is me," is one of the worst phrases ever. If you keep challenging your current narrative and always ask, "How can things be better?" you'll always have a positive attitude.

A positive attitude comes from accomplishing great feats and doing new things! It was an invigorating challenge to get to your fantasy place in life, right? Well, why was it so fun? It was a great challenge. It drew you out of your comfort zone because challenges and growth are naturally comfortable! Do you see this now? **Getting out of your comfort zone motivates you to do new things and inspires a great attitude for life.** It motivates you to keep what you love and blossom into greater loves.

## STEP 7 - FOCUS ON THE PROCESS, NOT THE CURRENT RESULTS

Getting out of your comfort zone is acknowledging that it's a process. Whenever you look at any accomplished individual, you'll find that they didn't start well in life. It took a while for them to have any financial freedom. They didn't have trust funds to lean on. They weren't given a job because of their wealthy dad or mom.

They focused on the process, not the current results. **They looked beyond their current capacity, what life currently is, and set their sights on a higher calling.** They set their sights on what it takes to reach their great destination and kept going. Zig Ziglar put it great by saying, *"When obstacles arise, you change your direction to reach your goal; you do not change your decision to get there."*

You made the original decision to do things like owning your own business, becoming a doctor, or raising a great family for some important reason, right? Well, if it was really that important to start, then why would something in the future keep you from finishing? Did you not think that problems would come up? Did you believe the pathway would be easy?

The pathway is never easy! It's always demanding, a struggle to get to what you want. This is why you...

## STEP 8 - EMBRACE THE STRUGGLE

You embrace the struggle. When Dr. Jordan Peterson, a clinical psychology and former Harvard professor, asks us to take responsibility for our lives, he acknowledges the reality of everyone's hardships, but says this,

> *"Making your life better means adopting a lot of responsibility, and that takes more effort and care than living stupidly in pain and remaining arrogant, deceitful, and resentful."* - (from his best-selling book, *12 Rules for Life*)

**If you don't embrace the struggle, you assume a lower level of living.** You shrink to adversity. You refuse to fight back when problems arise. You allow people to determine how you will live your life. You are pulled in every direction, making you a tireless cog who wakes up at 45, wondering where life took them. You're often ignored by society and become a shell of who you could be. Without the struggle and courage to persevere through tough times, you'll never have a positive attitude.

The tools are straightforward for us! Become an avid writer. Give yourself space to think about your why. Discover your passions and what you want your life to be like! Change your environment by whatever means necessary and keep challenging yourself to get out of your comfort zone! To be mentally tough and live with a great attitude for your life, you must embrace the struggle. **If you do these eight things, I will guarantee you'll always keep a positive attitude.**

# CHAPTER 7
# PROGRESSION | THE MOST IMPORTANT PART OF MOVING FORWARD

*"Most people who fail in their dream fail not from lack of ability, but from lack of commitment."* - Zig Ziglar

The struggle is real, boys and girls. You can't get around it and can't make everything easy. Trust fund babies even wake up one day in their 30s or 40s to discover that hard work is the only real key to accomplishing any achievements in life.

A passion must form, or else motivation can't take shape. The world's statements and decisions about us can't affect our perception. Our perspective must see opportunities, not impenetrable obstacles. With good goal-setting and a mindset for a grand vision of our future, we can persevere through any challenge.

In my opinion, the most crucial part of forming mental toughness is Progression. It's the very thing that helps keep you moving forward. **Because while anyone can persevere through challenges, that doesn't mean they're positively progressing.** It just means they can take punches all day. What good is it to take on the world's troubles if nothing positive comes from it?

Perseverance does not completely equal mental toughness. It's important, but progression matters so much more because **no matter what happens, we must find a way to positively move forward.** That's why the quote at the top of this chapter is so important. *"Most people who fail in their dream fail not from lack of ability but from lack of commitment."*

Your willingness to commit and never give up on whatever your goals or passions are will determine whether or not you accomplish them. You'll perfect it, whatever it is, and get there someday. It may take longer than you want, but you'll get there someday. For me, it took so much longer than I wanted! Do you think I wanted to wait until my 30s to figure out what I actually liked doing? And then, did you think I deliberately planned to have my businesses collapse in the recession and lose my job so I could find another head coaching job? Of course not! **But it's always worse when you decide to give up on your dreams and passions.**

## WHAT HAPPENS WHEN WE STOP MOVING? WHEN WE GIVE UP?

You lose self-worth whenever you give up on something you really wanted to happen. You spent years fantasizing about your life. You dreamed of an enduring, loving family, a career you enjoyed, and financial goals. After all these years, you finally had the boldness to start! You mustered up the necessary courage. But doesn't life seemingly know how to ruin a good moment? After some losses and insults to your ego, you fell on your sword and said, "Eh, I guess it was never meant to be."

You might be momentarily satisfied, but in the back of your mind, you're always going to think about this dream you had. You'll always have this as a continual failure in life. Why do you think you find middle-aged men returning to when they were high school athletes and when "times were simpler?" Well, it's because life got too complicated for them, and they never figured out what they were passionate about. They never had the continued boldness to run headfirst into accomplishing their passion.

**Anyone who has to look in the past for satisfaction has given up.** They've lost the pursuit of their passions and are now left to sit and wonder how it went wrong. When really, **the only thing that went wrong was they gave up.**

**When you stop moving forward, you get bitter about life.** Since life didn't work out well for you, then you are less optimistic about future events. You see an opportunity to try out for a tennis team at your new high school, for example, but you failed for years to make your former high school's team. You may have sat on the practice squad for years without any opportunity to play. Consequently, you let those negative moments cause you to become bitter and no longer try to thrive on your new school's tennis team.

What a loss! You now have no idea whether you could have really become good at tennis because you gave up! The world now has one less outstanding tennis player—what a shame.

This example works the same way for everything else in life. **When you're bitter, every opportunity looks bleak and bound to fail!** You end up playing mental games with yourself and convince yourself that nothing will work out how you'd like it to. Here are some examples of mental games and tricks we play with ourselves:

1. See that great-looking guy across the room? *There's no way he'd find you attractive.*

2. Your boss says there's an opportunity for promotion? *No, you're not good enough, and they don't really like you anyway.*
3. Is your son looking for a new hobby or activity to enjoy? *He's never been into cars. Why would he want to get under the hood with me and tinker around?*
4. Notice those old friends from college that accomplished their dreams? *There's no way they'd want to be friends with "little me" again. Look at where they are at!*

This goes back into the chapter on Perception. For the most part, **the only person telling you that you aren't good enough is YOU!** It seems stupid simple, but bitterness and loss of self-worth absolutely cripples people and keeps them from their potential. What a shame!

It gets worse. When you fully accept that your life can't get better, **you get resentful and envious of others.** You look at those old friends you had in college and think, "Ugh, why did they get to achieve all those cool things!?" You see social media posts of them getting a new puppy, buying that new house, or rocking that great, sculpted body. It all just makes your blood boil with rage. If you're not careful, this envy about your old friends from college spreads like cancer into your whole life. You start to resent everyone who's done better than you in life. You think that rich people shouldn't be given so much and that you should receive more assistance because life was unfair to you.

**You now define your life by your iniquities,** and boy, isn't that all too familiar today? I don't want to get political on you, but there's a growing amount of welfare given to people. There's a growing cry from the public to tax the rich more and for the government to give out more checks to people for just "being a citizen." I don't know about you, but I believe that **if everyone just decided to find their passion and pursued it with unrelenting discipline, we'd all be much happier.** We'd all at least be supportive of each other because we're all in the same pursuit.

Unfortunately, since you now define your life by your failures, you're bitter, resentful, and envious. **Now, you're a terrible example for the rest of us.** Let's say the worst happens, and you never achieve your goal. You just kept failing, decade after decade. If you just never stopped, you would still be an inspiration. People would say, *"Man, that guy is in his 50s, and he's still trying to be a rockstar. That's crazy."* That's what they'll say, but do you know what they secretly think? They think to themselves, *"I respect him for still trying. He's on stage, and I never had the guts."*

Remember, you don't pursue passions because of what people think. You chase them because it's YOUR passion! All the insults and complaining are from people that have given up or don't know their passions anyway! It's just like the old saying goes, *"Misery loves company."* And when you're not part of that company, it really pisses them off.

Do you see how this is a big snowball effect? We started with a simple example of a young high schooler who never seized their chance as a tennis player. Several years later, he's quickly turned into a man who asks for undeserving handouts from the government.

## "COACH P, WHEN IS QUITTING OKAY?"

People quit doing things all the time; in some cases, it's actually for their benefit. They begin developing a skill, thinking that this is the skill they want to flourish in, but ultimately, it's not something they're passionate about. When I owned a construction and sporting goods business, I enjoyed starting something new and developing great relationships with people. This was fun and exciting!

Do you know what wasn't exciting? The actual work of running a business. After a year of work, you face many frustrations you didn't realize would happen. You see what it's *really like* to manage employees. You learn how much you need to set aside in taxes (and quickly become a libertarian). You face challenges from every direction, and for me, after the newness wore off, I realized that growing businesses was not my passion.

I discovered that I was passionate about teaching others how to thrive and be successful. After all the activities and interests I pursued for decades after school, I ultimately discovered that teaching and mentoring were my natural longing. I didn't want to see my businesses fail during the 2008 recession, but you know what, I haven't tried to replicate it now. **I've focused my attention.** I kept my eyes on what I was genuinely passionate about and quit pursuing anything else I found didn't bring me sustained joy. This is important: *"sustained joy."*

**When you realize that something isn't your passion, quit immediately.** Just don't stop something too quickly. **Momentary hardship does not mean you weren't passionate.** Everyone deals with challenges. As I mentioned earlier in the book, I recently took on a head coaching job at a high school in Florida. Our first season was probably my worst coaching season ever. We didn't win a single game. There were a lot of hurdles and challenges to overcome, and even though our team mightily improved, we still had a 0-10 record to show for it.

Not a great start for the brand new head coach! I've been at this for a long time now, and **I know that these seasons happen.** You have disappointments, and you have struggles. It was a struggle for the entire season! Do you think I'm just going to throw in the towel and say that I'm a washed-up coach who doesn't know anything anymore? Of course not! **If I give up, then I'm no longer choosing to progress.** I'm choosing to settle for less, which starts the negative snowball effect.

There is one caveat for deciding to quit a passion, and it's a caveat that our founding fathers and grandparents likely had to do. **They sacrificed their desires to provide a more excellent life for their children and others.** Let's think about this. Back in the 1800s, there was a massive migration of people to the United States from Europe. Over 32 million people found new homes in a place called "America," where there was an opportunity for a better life. The United States was once popularly called "The Land of Opportunity." These people would cram into big wooden ships, spend months at sea with infants and families, and venture out to an unknown land with unknown possibilities.

There was much uncertainty, but they were confident they could build a life of opportunity for themselves and, more importantly, their children. Many of our great, great grandparents broke their backs and sacrificed their own desires to provide an opportunity for their children and grandchildren to thrive in this new land. Instead of selfishly spoiling themselves, they left everything for their children to make a better life for themselves.

You see families everywhere making this sacrifice, especially single mothers. Single mothers are dealt an unfortunate hand by marrying an awful man and often bearing children at very early, unwise times. Instead of abandoning the child and moving on to whatever they wanted for themselves, they make a very noble sacrifice. They decide to sacrifice their wants for their child's needs, so they can hopefully move on and build a better life.

This is why you find so many NFL football players and NBA stars giving their most profound love and admiration to their mothers. Many of these mothers are single mothers. These kids made it to an elite level with their talents and wisely understood that it couldn't be possible without their mothers' many sacrifices. It's a gigantic, crippling problem in this country and worldwide. Fathers and men everywhere are selfishly abandoning their responsibility and giving up on the noblest goal they can pursue, mentoring the next generation to be better than them.

**Sometimes, you can't quit something even if you don't like it.** This is not a bad thing. You don't quit because **the cause is too great to run away from.** This is why you find dissatisfied couples staying together because they know it's dramatically better for their children to stay married and "tough it out." You may disagree, but that's what the statistics show! And hey, maybe the marriage can get better because you didn't quit.

You can't stop progressing no matter how your life looks or what happens. If you get anything from this book, please understand this. You will find that anyone who's accomplished anything never stopped pursuing their passions. They never stopped setting goals for themselves. **They always maintained a mindset of growth.**

## WHAT DOES PROGRESS LITERALLY LOOK LIKE?

There's one thing I wanted to make sure to do before leaving this chapter, and it's to walk you through how to progress, literally. People are taught all the time how to start things. There are conferences, events, books, and online courses about "starting a business," "learning how to cook," or "learning a new language."

What isn't explained so much is the reality of what progress literally looks like. What does it actually look like to set goals? Not just initial goals (we already covered that), but after accomplishing those goals, how do we create new goals? How do we always ensure forward movement, even amid immense struggles? How do we keep ourselves focused without getting distracted by other things? 50% of small businesses fail in five years, 50% of first marriages eventually fail, and only 7% of New Year's resolutions are kept. It's obvious we're not figuring this out!

**What must be addressed is the amount of detail needed for setting goals.** I find most people of all ages don't understand what it truly takes to set clear, defined goals. It's much more detailed than most people realize. I use the example of purchasing a car in my classes in high school. This is often a purchase that's made by their parents or by them at this age. So to help them, I educate them on all the steps that are truly necessary for purchasing a car. Here's how I run them through the steps:

1. First of all, **when do you want a new car?** I know "now" is the clear answer, but you can't just get a car "now." You must define a timeframe for when to

accomplish a goal. Before you take action, this must be written down.

2. **Why do I want or need a new car?** If you're looking for a "new" car, there must be a specific reason why that is. New is very different from used. Is it that important to get a "new" car? Plenty of people get new cars, but very few "need" new cars. Clearly write down why this is.
3. **What type of car? Make, Model, Year?** An obvious question, but you still need to write it down and be clear. Salespeople are great at getting you to buy something nice but not ultimately what you want. You can't stand firm with what you want if you don't write it down.
4. **What's the cost of the car?** Everyone must have a budget, so balance the wants and needs you have with your new or used vehicle with this ultimate number.
5. **How much money do you have on hand?** Don't lie to yourself. How much money do you actually have right now? You probably don't have enough to get everything you want. You might have enough for a car, but is it really what you'll enjoy having for over a decade? Or is this more temporary than a decade?
6. **Will I finance or purchase outright?** Both have pros and cons, but write down what you would like to do.

Now, here's what this all looks like written out into a plan:

**Goal Defined:** 10 months to have funds available.

**Purchase Date:** 10 months from whatever day it is today. If today is November 10th, then our goal is to purchase a car by September 10th next year.

**What's the Car?:** Purchasing a car, a used Ford Escape that's 6-7 years old, with low mileage of 75,000 miles or under. Royal Blue, black interior.

**How Much Money?:** Cost $9,000. Have $4,000 on hand and can save $500.00 per month. The completion date is purchasing a car for cash.

<u>Action Steps</u>

**Months 1-9:** Save $500.00 per month.

You can break this down into bite-size terms for success: $500 divided by four weeks = $125.00 per week OR $125.00 divided by seven days = $17.86 per day. So if you work a $14 per hour job, you can fund this car by putting aside a couple of hours of what you earn daily at work.

**Month 10:** Begin searching for a car with your predetermined specifications and purchase it!

See how detailed we had to be? It might have blown some of your minds to read this breakdown. Some of you have reacted by saying, "Booo, this is boring. This is too much work. Do you really need to go into this detail?"

Let me ask, do you *really* want your goal to happen? Whether you like it or not, it requires this kind of detail. This is what the best and brightest do. We can either see what's required and do it, or we can accept mediocrity. Which would you prefer?

**Plans will never go as planned.** There will always be unpredictable things that get in the way. For this example, you could look at how the automobile industry in the last year has seen a dramatic price hike. You'll find reports showing how new car prices have risen by over 12% since last year. So if you were looking to buy that car in ten months, you would now have to wait two more months at least. You could be waiting longer because the price of everything is going up! You would likely have been tempted to skip a month for unexpected expenses elsewhere.

As in this example, these obstacles are genuinely tremendous and sometimes very difficult to overcome. You lose a job while trying to save. You have an unexpected pregnancy and now need to find another $1,000 per month in income. **This is okay because this is life.** Obstacles like this happen to everyone trying to make their passions come alive. So will you face these challenges head-on?

I think you know the answer. MOVE FORWARD AND MAKE PROGRESS!

# CHAPTER 8
# PERSEVERE AND "YOU'LL MAKE IT ALL RIGHT!"

*"Perhaps the unwelcome event you've encountered is just an opportunity to help you know how to stand up stronger."* - Dan Miller

Do you know how in most movies, there's a point where it seems all hope is lost? The lead character seems to have trouble finding out how to solve the problem, and she doesn't know where to turn next. She may have already discovered how to solve it, but it's too late. The odds for success seem so staggering that it looks like an absolute fantasy, a pipe dream!

Then all of a sudden, with most cinematic movies, there's the ultimate moment where the lead character's big break comes. A friend shows up from nowhere, the antagonist makes a mistake, or the lead character sees a golden opportunity they boldly seize. The lead character continues to persevere, even when all hope is lost. They're always looking at the opportunities to reach the end objective.

What we find in most successful films is a clear illustration of perseverance. It's the great struggle to surpass all odds and accomplish what you'd love to do. Even in unwelcome events, as Dan Miller stated, we're looking for the opportunity to stand up stronger. Folks, without this lesson, you can't make it anywhere in life.

## LIFE LOOKS LIKE A LOT OF DISAPPOINTMENT, HONESTLY

I'm 65 years old, and most of you reading this book will be much younger than me. High school students, young athletes in college, football coaches, and parents alike will read this book. Since most of you will have fewer gray hairs, I feel I can give good insight on perseverance because I've literally stayed alive for over 60 years!

There's been so many close to my heart that I've lost. The first person I can think of in life was my father. At 27 years old, far younger than any man should lose his father, I no longer got to see him due to brain cancer. The following year, my younger brother traumatically passed away, and I was almost hope-stricken. Two close people in my family having their lives taken away in a snap? It nearly broke me.

I'm honestly grateful on some level that I was still drinking alcohol because, man, in some weird way, it probably helped get me through this depressing point in life. It's part of the reason why when I was 29 years old, after losing my father and younger brother in the previous two years, I lost my job with Conveyor Systems. Year after year, in my late twenties, shockingly depressing things happened in my life.

It's never fun losing jobs, and I've lost many. Losing businesses hurts even more because they feel like your own children! The list goes on and on as my life has passed. Close friends and relatives died. Two of my sons died in their twenties. Other businesses failed due to bankruptcy and poor personal management of the companies. Life is hard.

While I'd love to tell you some elusive secret to avoid the world's perils, it's just unavoidable. **You can't find a success story without a breakdown.** From famous athletes to popular celebrities or troublesome childhood stories, you can't find a life where nothing went wrong. Many times, people have horrible backstories.

Everyone deals with pain and struggle. Athletes struggle to improve themselves way beyond any natural talent. They start off having natural abilities to catch a ball or run fast, but they need to train their butts off to get to the highest level possible. For most people, the highest level of sports they reach isn't anywhere near receiving scholarships and paid salaries.

Parents struggle to maintain sanity when one, two, or five kids are being raised at a time. No matter how many books you read, nothing can truly prepare you for raising a child. It's a living, breathing organism you're tasked with raising to become the most fantastic human being possible. It's an insane task that we all attempt to do. Most of us are lucky and thankful if our kids end up just being normal!

Everyone struggles with managing their lives. I can't tell you how many times I've heard people complain about their work, lack of fun, or the lousy people they have in their lives. Appropriately managing everything we handle is an ultimate struggle that few of us are very good at. I even struggle with keeping things balanced in my life!

Beyond just living, unpredictable things come up along the way. Car accidents, divorces, major clients leaving your business, long-term illnesses, and so much more. Good people are constantly dealt significant blows to their life that seem out of nowhere. The big question for all of this is, how do we cope with life's troubles? How do we keep ourselves from going crazy when the world is so chaotic?

## IT STARTS WITH THANKFULNESS

I started this chapter with a negative tone, but if you consider your circumstances, you're probably doing fine. You're not sad or deeply depressed about life, but you're not content with being just "fine." And you shouldn't be! Life wasn't meant for just living a "fine" life. It was meant for so much more! While I've had so much tragedy happen, and many of you could be living in an awful place, I have had plenty of great successes and breakthroughs. I've helped plenty of my students and friends be able to break through or rethink their circumstances for the better too!

First and foremost, **we need to be thankful.** This first point might surprise you. The very reason you're reading this book is that you are finding something dissatisfactory about your life, right? So why should we start by being thankful for something we dislike?

**Many people have it worse than you.** Please don't skip this point because it's vital! Especially as Americans, we get so caught up in our own little worlds. All the problems and troubles and issues we face seem like the greatest grievances we've ever dealt with. From long traffic lines to divorce from your spouse, times can get hard, but not as traumatically difficult as the rest of the world. If we just looked beyond ourselves, we'd find other cities, states, and countries with far more significant problems.

**By starting with thankfulness, we get our minds in the right starting place to persevere through our troubles.** If we can't find a single thing to be thankful for or appreciative of, then we're never going to see the bright side! We'll never face a troublesome situation and find a lesson in it. We will fail to see how we can fix a problem, and the problem will continue to come again and again. If we can't get good at being thankful, we'll always find ourselves in a doom loop of despair.

How do you get good at being thankful? You can start by saying, "Wow, at least I'm born in America, where I don't have to walk for miles every day to get water." It's humbling to think about. It gives a sense of appreciation for the blessing you didn't deserve from birth.

Look around today! Many states are struggling with finances, employment issues, inflation and you name it. My original home state of Illinois is on the verge of bankruptcy and taxes are sky high. I know right now, I can find great blessings living in Florida, where we don't pay any state payroll taxes. There is always something or somewhere that has it worse than you do.

We must also **consider where we came from.** We get so caught up in our current state of sorrow sometimes, but let's remind ourselves about the past troubles we've persevered from! Remember that bad habit you had when growing up or in your 20s? Now it's not a thing; you should be grateful for that! Or how about when you wet the bed sometimes? When you needed your "blankie" to get through the night? When you were just starting to play football and didn't know anything about drawing up plays or proficient tackling? **If you dig deep enough, there is always something you persevered and came back better from!**

The last part of thankfulness is **seeing the growth opportunities ahead of you.** This goes back to chapter 5 on clearly seeing a great future ahead of you. If you're a 14-year-old kid who wants to become great at football, you still have a handful of years ahead of you to bulk up your strength, get smart about football plays and become an all-star athlete! The growth opportunities are always best the younger you are in age.

Let's say you're in your mid-40s, though, and plenty of years have gone by. Well, how's your health? Are you still able to move around and exercise? If so, you can still change your body and be proud of how you look and feel! Or how about if you're in your mid-50s and always wanted to learn a language or play an instrument? Well, you still know how to talk, right? And you probably still have strength in your fingers to play an instrument, too, right? Then the opportunity for learning and growth IS THERE!

Be thankful that you even have the opportunity and capabilities to learn new things! I see many people a couple of decades younger than me looking so sad. It's like they're ready to die. Life gave them quite a few wrenches, and they haven't made themselves into someone they're proud of. **What's even more depressing, though, is that no one is telling these people it's hopeless except for themselves.** These downtrodden folks in their 60s, 50s, 40s, and heck even 30s have all decided that it's not worth it anymore.

**What I'm telling you is that it's always worth it.** I could have thrown in the towel so many times! Do you think I like the fact that I've been fired from coaching jobs due to finances or poor team performances? Of course not! Do you think I enjoyed how terrible the recession went for our family? Do I still have moments where I cry to myself in the car about the fact that my two sons died in their 20s and will never have the opportunity to create a great life for themselves? It's depressing how cruel life can be!

But then, as I drive, I see that my car works well. I see I'm still married (and happily, I might add)! This means my wife and I have beaten the odds and persevered through everything to stay happily together. And as I drive, I notice a homeless person just camped out at an intersection holding a sign for money, and the woman looks to be my age. I think, "Wow, I'm so glad I have a house. Thank God." And suddenly, the turmoil and tribulation can fade because I found a way to be thankful for my past, present, and future. Be grateful, and you'll be mentally tough.

## TRACK YOUR PROGRESS AND SEE THE DAILY BABY STEPS

Once you've become thankful, it's time to act. I've said this before, and I'll repeat it, **write down what needs to happen in your life!** Get out a journal, calendar, or to-do list and write down the plan of action. Even if these seem like baby steps, it's still progress, and you're still moving forward instead of backward!

It reminds me of a classic Bill Murray comedy from the early '90s called "*What About Bob?*". For any Gen Zers reading this book, I encourage you to check out this movie. It's about a very nervous, paranoid man (Bill Murray) who works with a psychologist that gives him life instructions that blow his mind. As a result, Bill Murray follows this man around everywhere and ruins his family's weekend vacation.

The lesson the psychologist gave him was a series of books that he wrote titled *Baby Steps*. The principle was that anyone could improve and be a little proud of themselves by simply taking baby steps of development. Murray jokingly mocks this point with his humor, but the principle is fundamental! If you just focus on nailing down one thing today or one thing consistently this week, then you won't overwhelm yourself by fixing everything in your life right now! So, **take baby steps and focus on one thing at a time.**

By writing down these steps and tracking the results, you're giving yourself more reasons to be thankful and encouraging you to keep moving forward, no matter what tribulations get in the way. This is why it's so good to **keep the focus on the written plan.** It's tough to do this when it's not written down, and you don't remind yourself of it daily. Life has a way of making things more difficult when you're trying to take extraordinary steps forward. Keep the focus on the plan.

## WATCH OUT FOR THESE CHALLENGES & SURPASS THEM

No matter how amazing we think we are, challenges will always arise, typically growing in complexity. While you focus on your written plan and take baby steps to grow, I encourage you to be watchful for the three main categories of challenges you will face.

**You will face literal, tangible challenges.** These are the most obvious ones. Examples of these include getting a flat tire, running out of hot water, or having a flight delayed, causing you to be late for the connecting flight. They are the physical limitations that get in the way of what you'd like to accomplish. These are actually the most manageable challenges to persevere past.

**For the most part, you can't control or limit these challenges.** They just simply come up, and we must deal with them as they come up. Now, if you can limit or control them, then you have the opportunity to learn how to do this, and it never happens again! But when these unpredictable challenges come, we persevere through them in two main ways; understanding that they are uncontrollable and quickly solving the controllable problems.

If you maintain an understanding that uncontrollable things happen throughout life, you'll be much more peaceful when, for instance, a golf ball flings off the course and cracks your car windshield. It's a sense of calm that says, "You know, this doesn't happen every day, and this too shall pass." The wisdom comes from an old scripture verse in 2 Corinthians 4:17, which says, *"For our light and momentary troubles are achieving for us an eternal glory that far outweighs them all."* **The keyword here is "momentary."**

Most of these unforeseen problems are momentary. So if it's momentary, there shouldn't be any reason to get yourself in a temper tantrum, right? I've found that many people have a hard time getting past these issues. Have you ever met someone who thinks that if the worst could happen, it will? They seem to believe the world is against them, and anything they try that's out of their comfort zone probably won't work?

Let's call these people the "Self-Defeating Prophesiers." Anything you propose for them to do, they'll respond with a comment like, "Yeah…I just don't know if it'll work." They may even be smart with the response and say, "Well, I don't have experience with that, and I've heard bad things could happen. So, I'll just play it safe." They could respond even more passively and say, "Yeah, sure, let's give it a whirl, but we'll see if it works."

Do you see the problem in this communication? **How can you persevere and thrive in life if you always think it won't work out for you?** Do you think Elon Musk is working on his next spaceship, thinking it won't work? Do you think Lebron James invested in Blaze Pizza (a chain of high-quality, assembly-line pizza places), thinking he wouldn't make a return? **Anyone successful in life thinks optimistically about their opportunities.** There's room for skepticism and critiquing plans, but if you never boldly and confidently seize opportunities, you'll always be sitting on the sidelines. You'll never be in the game! Physical, literal limitations will come up, but you've got to be calm and cool enough to keep moving.

**You will face emotional challenges too.** These challenges mainly deal with fear. We all have emotional bents and tendencies. While some people are nervous about how people think about them, I get very gun-shy whenever I try new things. It happened with this book! This book was made possible because I had a trusted advisor and friend who did much of the heavy lifting for me. I followed his lead, and if he weren't there to help, I'd still be on page one!

That's actually one of the ways you combat emotional challenges. **You follow someone's lead and guidance.** If someone is more confident in a skill, just follow them and gain your confidence through your experiences with them. For instance, if you want to get good at playing volleyball but you are not great at it, it would be helpful to make friends with people who are confident in volleyball and already know how to play well. That friend would hopefully invite you into their group; therefore, you gain more confidence through them.

Whenever nothing is keeping you from doing something, it's probably an emotional issue. You fear something, like how people will react, how good it will work out, how badly others work it out. It could be any reason! The two main ways to combat emotional challenges are first acknowledging the emotion and then leaning on your support group.

Acknowledging the emotion keeps you from feeling like it's a mystery why you can't get started or can't seem to make any progress. Emotions shut you off from sound advice and keep you from being open. When you acknowledge a feeling out loud to yourself, it's no longer concealed. It's out in the open and can now be addressed! The best way to address any emotional issue is with trusted advisors, friends, and family members. You've built trust with these people to hear sound wisdom and criticism; from them, you'll come up with methods to get past whatever emotional problem keeps you from your potential!

**Finally, you'll face spiritual issues.** What I mean is that each of us has a human spirit. We have motivations within us to grow and desire to do things in life. It's hard to put into words, but it's as if we're born with these callings or passions. While positive spiritual truths exist, we also have debilitating, deep issues that plague us. We have rooted scars due to years and years of something happening to us.

Bullying is an excellent example of this. Kids that spend their lives in public schools are incessantly bullied by their fellow students. They are at significant risk of lackluster grades, lousy occupations, forming weaker social relationships, and making bad decisions in life. What's even sadder is how bullying now causes rising suicide rates among adolescents. According to the United Health Foundation, suicide is the second-leading cause of death for ages 10 - 24. This means these kids have been bullied and ridiculed so much that, on a spiritual level, they believe their life will never be better and it isn't worth it anymore.

And for those of us who boldly continue to live on, we're stuck with spiritual problems that keep us down without even knowing it! You might feel like you struggle to make a good income, not because you're lazy or unintelligent, but because your entire family has never been good at managing money. As a result, you've learned deep, crippling habits and thought processes that, unfortunately, make you seem not to have enough money to go by. You've been subconsciously trained to manage money poorly, and it's time you and others get past these deep, spiritual issues.

You'll want to seek counsel from your friends and family, but I encourage you to spend time reading and personally investing in outside sources too. Whether you know what giant limitation you have or not, you'll grow and flourish by feeding yourself with uplifting, positive content. Podcasts are an excellent source for this! My podcast's sole purpose (*The Mental Toughness Podcast with Coach P*) is to provide people with a motivating and uplifting message every single day. That way, you'll always have someone in your corner cheering you on and challenging you to be better than before!

Books are also a great source for this, along with lectures, informative YouTube videos, and interviews with people you admire. You're essentially altering how your mind thinks and looks at the world. Just for your information, this isn't a snap-of-a-finger process! As a result of years and years of investing in your well-being and self-improvement, it will be undeniable that you'll change.

Going back to the poor money management example, you will ultimately become a great money manager if you want. You can be the one person in your family who thrives financially! Here's what it will take:

1. An enormous amount of reading and studying to see how the best people do it.
2. A new discipline to learn how to save and not spend. This will be utterly foreign to you because you haven't seen any personal examples from your family.
3. You'll need the backbone not to be tempted to spend money whenever you start saving.
4. You'll need to be watchful of your family members. Now that they see you have money, they'll likely find ways to get some extra dough from you. You'll become an easy target for moochers.
5. You'll need to do all of this for years upon years. To radically change your financial well-being for the long haul? It's a lifetime process, but so worth it!

As you might imagine, this is just a summarized list. It could require counseling or temporary sacrifices to get you on the right track! When it comes to a serious problem in your life, your attitude should be to do whatever it takes. There's one great story I have in mind of a man who did whatever it took to live his dream.

## THE LEGENDARY *RUDY* STORY

Daniel Ruettiger, more commonly known as "Rudy," grew up in Illinois and dreamed of playing football for the Notre Dame Fighting Irish. He wasn't a huge guy, standing 5′6″; for football standards, that's very small. That's especially true because he only weighed 165 lbs coming out of high school! After a couple of years in the Navy, he attempted to apply to Notre Dame, but they rejected him due to poor grades in high school. What Rudy didn't know was that he had dyslexia. He found this out when he went to the college next door to Notre Dame.

Notre Dame ended up rejecting Rudy's application four times. As you might imagine, he's constantly dealing with doubt and frustration. All he knew was that this was the opportunity to try and play for Notre Dame's football team, so he would make his greatest effort. He worked out an insane amount and got himself as big as possible, along with studying all day and all night. Finally, on the fifth try, he got accepted into Notre Dame, and that fall, he made it onto the scout team.

At this time, Notre Dame was one of the top college football teams in the country. During the 1960s, when Rudy was placed on the scout team, the Notre Dame Fighting Irish football team was ranked as a top 10 school six years in a row. The fact that Rudy was even on the scout team for his height and build was amazing to imagine. Most everyone is towering over him since he's only 5′6″!

For some people, this would be good enough. But Rudy had his dream still very much alive! He was so close to his end goal that he would stick it out until it couldn't be possible anymore. He stayed on their scout team for two seasons, getting pummeled by the starting squad, taking hits all day. He would receive no playtime on the field, and he couldn't even suit up with the team since he was on their scout team. As his senior year wound down, Rudy seemed to come to terms with the fact that he'd never suited up on the field.

That's until the last home game of the season. Rudy had built such an excellent reputation with the team and his coaches that the head coach decided to have Rudy suit up for his last home game as a senior. Not only did Rudy go on the sidelines, but he also went on the field for three plays! And on the final play of his very short career, he rushed the quarterback and sacked him to finish the game. In this moment of immense glory, Rudy was lifted on the shoulders of his players and carried off the field, being the first player ever to be carried off the field in the Notre Dame football stadium.

This story is a hallmark example of mental toughness and perseverance. Rudy had to keep his head high and be thankful for every opportunity he still had. At first, he had the chance to go to college next door to Notre Dame, then he made it into Notre Dame, and with each small step toward this gigantic goal, he kept being thankful that he was even there. No matter how many obstacles got in his way, he was appreciative even to be where he was.

He tracked his success through better and better grades and by monitoring his performance on the football field. He also had significant influences in his life to help support him and encourage him to keep going, even when things looked insanely tough. And all along the way, he didn't let the physical, emotional, or spiritual limitations keep him from this fantastic dream. As a result of all this effort, he can now move on and know that he gave his all. Even if he never got to play on the field or get a sack, he still would have been proud of himself. Anyone would be proud of themselves for persevering and trying their absolute best for their goals.

That's what perseverance is all about. That's what Mental Toughness is all about.

# CHAPTER 9
# THE SECRET P THAT NO ONE LIKES

*"Don't sweat the small stuff, and everything is small stuff."* - Zig Ziglar

Have you ever committed to something, like an event or an extra assignment, and then found it difficult to fulfill it? You thought you could handle the additional responsibility, but sooner or later, you're no longer able to adequately deliver on the task like you said you would? Are you looking to accomplish something that seems too big to handle?

What you and I experience is something everyone experiences. An emotional reaction occurs from the first moment you take responsibility for something. It's called "pressure," and pressure is everywhere. With every effort to accomplish a task, there will be pressure. You will genuinely be mentally tough when you understand this truth and use pressure to your advantage. Using pressure to push you past adversity is something every great person learns to do. Because let's face it, pressure is life!

Well, a good life, that is. Too often, pressure is associated with stress. Tell you what, the next time you're given something to do or be responsible for, watch how your body reacts. Your muscles may begin to tense up for seemingly no reason. Your back and neck feel sore because you've been hunched over, racking your brain over whatever problem you try to solve. You experience headaches frequently, and if one more thing goes wrong, you're just not sure you can get past it. That's horrible stress that many people experience regularly.

In a 2017 study done by the American Psychological Association, **approximately 60% of the US population is living with continual, significant stress.** Some say their source of stress comes from money (62%), their work status (61%), or the violence and crime in their city (51%). These same Americans are quoted saying, *"The United States is at the lowest point they can remember in its history."*

But this was in 2017, before the multi-year pandemic that spread across the entire world. This same organization did another study during the month of August 2020. It's only gotten worse. The report states, *"Nearly 8 in 10 adults (78%) say the coronavirus pandemic is a significant source of stress in their life."* People were out of jobs for several months, older folks and loved ones passed away earlier than we hoped, schooling was terrible to navigate through as parents, and tensions rose exponentially over how we should all be reacting to this whole thing. It was likely the most traumatizing, life-threatening stress some people have ever experienced in this country.

I have to be honest, I was nervous. I'm in my later 60's, in the most threatened part of the population. In the first couple of months, just like everyone else, I didn't know how to react or what to do properly. I wore masks, and I did my best to distance myself socially. Heck, almost everyone was bent out of shape on some level. I know I live in Florida, but everyone my age was worried about this thing! For all of us, the pressure to continue to show up to work, make payments on cars, and keep living life "semi-normally" was a lot to bear.

Throughout the pandemic, I was stressed about the fact that my passion could be taken away. Children where be home schooled and football programs put on hold. Imagine my very passion in life taken away because of a pandemic, something out of my control? Would I be starting over again at 63 years old?

After the first couple of months, though, I reminded myself of the Zig Ziglar quote at the top of this chapter. *"Don't sweat the small stuff, and everything is small stuff."* I remember a couple of decades ago, hearing Zig Ziglar myself at one of his speaking engagements and feverishly consuming his books. The man had an elegant, simple way of explaining how to live an accomplished and content life. There's a certain calm if you live life like this, to not sweat the small stuff. Don't you find people who don't get stressed about little annoyances usually don't get stressed when big things happen?

So after the first couple of months, when it no longer looked like the pandemic would be a "two-week isolation," I decided to step out and continue living as normally as possible. Of course, I wasn't crashing weddings and clubbing! I kept doing what I wanted and needed to do, though. I chose not to "sweat it." I decided that I couldn't let anything threaten me from living a life I'm proud to live, even if it meant risking my life.

This calm is something I'd like to teach you. All of us need to do a better job at managing stress and pressure in life. Can't you just look around and feel the tension in this country? Yeah, bad things are happening, but as long as we can handle the pressure and stress we can control, we'll do fine without sweating the other stuff!

## PRESSURE VS. STRESS

First, we must distinguish the differences between pressure and stress because many people think they are the same. If you're stressed about something, you probably feel the weight or pressure to alleviate your stress. For example, if your parents pressure you to find a "safer job," then you might be stressed out due to this pressure. Are you following me?

The reason why we have such a hard time with pressure is because we typically didn't ask for it. Nobody's consciously looking to stress themselves out! As a result of just living life, we find ourselves being pushed or "pressured" by the circumstances around us. Pressure arises everywhere, from the big stuff, like presenting the quarterly report to your boss, to the small stuff, like knowing what you want to order in line.

Since many people aren't comfortable under any pressure, they tense up and paralyze themselves on some level. We stammer, have trouble finding the words to say, and even freeze, paralyzed under pressure and fearing the circumstance. Many of us see all these issues as problems we can't control. We're stressed because we always like having control, and once it's threatened, it's a race to fix it now!

This is how we instinctively react. "Oh, my schedule changed at work, and now I have to find a new babysitter?" I'm stressed. "Oh, I got in a small wreck, and the insurance isn't covering it?" I'm stressed. "Oh, my kid isn't learning math easily and still wets the bed?" I'm stressed. We quickly throw this label on the many issues that come up, and it seemingly ruins any bliss our life could have. Instead of maintaining control over our emotions, the stress and anxiety controls us.

What's crazy about this is that we can easily change our circumstances. As you've already read, there are three phases of achievement that we all must have to attain mental toughness. By (1) finding your passion and (2) setting goals for your life, we (3) maintain a great mindset for growth. We're mentally tough. We don't allow the pressures or stresses of life to keep us down.

This doesn't mean we're unstoppable. Anything that takes you out of your comfort zone will give you pressure, which leads to discomfort, and we're not very tolerant of discomfort in the United States. We'll do anything (and I mean anything) to avoid pain or anything uncomfortable. There are small social nuances, like seeing someone you'd rather not talk to at a gathering and walking into another room. There are also more pivotal discomforts we avoid, like refusing to tell your spouse that you've been unfaithful to them.

## WE SETTLE FOR LACKLUSTER

Do you know where I find this "pressure avoidance" the most? With people's jobs. I see so many people just settling for where they work. They are unhappy about their job, but they don't even look for what would interest them. Even if they aren't "unhappy," they are disengaged in the workplace. They clock in and clock out, and that's it! The Gallup polling research backs this up, where in a 2021 study, they found that 64% of US employees were disengaged in the workplace. It's even worse internationally, with 80% of workers not finding purpose and fulfillment in their work. That is a LOT of people! **If over 150 million US citizens are working right now, that**

**means over 96 million would love to have another, better job.**

Ladies and gentlemen, do you realize how insane this is? I rack my brain about this frequently. I emphatically tell my students how important it is to find your passion sooner than later. Otherwise, you'll just take whatever job "gives you the most money," and that's never the best job.

But you know, this might not be that insane to people. Remember, most people are disengaged in the workplace. We live in a world where the "can't wait until Friday" attitude lives strong. People rage on at parties on the weekends or simply find as many excuses as possible to live a lazy weekend. When everyone has the same mediocre experience, it doesn't seem so odd that we hate our jobs because everyone does!

But readers, by this point, you know better. Something needs to change! You've read eight chapters of this book, so you can't accept another year at a terrible job. Please, pursue your passions! Try out tons of things to determine what you're even passionate about! You can be like Jill Donovan, founder of Rustic Cuff, who, each year, dives deep into a new hobby to help her discover new passions. With this annual ritual, she learned the skill of bracelet and cuff making. She got better and better and found a genuine love for giving these cufflinks out as gifts to friends and family far and wide. Now, she has a thriving multi-million dollar business with celebrities like Oprah, Michael Buble, and Britney Spears. She's got a whole list of big-name celebrities photographed wearing her cufflinks that she gifted them! **This all started because she was willing to give an interest a serious try.**

That's all it takes. Just give it a try. Where's the pressure? Where's the stress? The anxiety of trying new things plagues so many people, but all these reasons only truly stem from one source; what other people will think.

Social pressures are key to silencing the weak of heart. This problem has crippled billions of workers who want to go to a new line of work but are nervous it won't work out. They're worried about what people will think of them if they fail. It keeps our children from trying a new sport or art form because their peers might make fun of them. They might embarrass themselves, and middle school is embarrassing enough (according to my children)!

We create so many excuses in our minds that the stress of pursuing our passions is too much. In reality, where is the pressure? Where is the stress when we stop listening to all the haters in the world?

Furthermore, all pressure is not negative pressure. Negative pressure indeed does exist. I experienced this when I started a couple of businesses decades ago. These companies ultimately failed because of the recession, but honestly, they would've likely failed even if a recession didn't happen. We started taking on more significant projects than we could handle, a common mistake for companies. We tried to maintain it, but it wore down our abilities to do what we needed in the business and our own lives. The pressure to deliver for all these clients we committed to was genuinely too much for our current team. Ergo, there is such a thing as negative pressure.

I can remember the pressure of making the decision to go to my present position at Central High School. Everyone I talked with told me I was making a mistake. They unanimously told me it was a bad move going to a school with a losing culture and declining numbers. "You should just stay with what I have!"

The local sports media even got involved, stating that I took over the toughest rebuild in the state of Florida.

Would I be happy with the challenge? I had to make a decision and as I always preach to others, what other people think doesn't matter, it's your life, it's your challenge. Make a decision and don't look back. And friends, I can truly say that after only one year, a season where we didn't win a single game, the worst rebuild in the state of Florida has turned out to be the best position I have ever had. **Don't let other people's perspective become your reality.**

Positive pressure is when you decide to take action on an ambitious goal, and the longing to succeed forces you to success. Any goal can be ambitious, even if it seems small. For instance, if you are a young man looking to improve your ability to talk to women, there's a simple method to doing this. You just start talking to more women. Men think that it's not that simple, but in reality, it is.

Any man who becomes good at talking to women, and eventually finds a good wife, has learned to use pressure to their advantage. They have discovered what women care about. They have improved their ability just to listen and respond with empathy. They have become more humorous, eventually mastering the art of being a "kidder." They have also looked to become the best version of themselves so they are more attractive.

In this example, we took a seemingly small goal (getting good at talking to women), identified the various pressures around this (not looking stupid or weak), and found ways to improve performance (learning skills in listening, humor, and ownership of one's life). You will find the positive pressures are all around us, but we too often see them as negative. This goes back into the Mindset phase of the three phases of achievement. The pressure to perform well at a job could be negative if you hate it, but it can be positive if you like it. Even if you hate your job, this pressure is positive because you can use your good performance in a bad environment to make you attractive to the jobs you really want.

The pressure to raise great children could be damaging if your kids keep acting up and you keep telling yourself that you "hate kids." It could be a positive pressure, however, when you challenge yourself to raise good children and stay with your spouse. The bar is set quite low for being a good parent because many bad parents are out there. Even if only 2% of the population considers themselves bad parents, you see these bad parents regularly. You see these bad parents through their children! Since I'm a teacher and coach, I see this very often. If you always try and never give up on being a good parent, you'll be better than most.

The negative pressure mindset is found in all income scales and every walk of life. Poor families are nervous to try anything because they don't want their lives to be worse, but is it better to settle for a lackluster life? Is it better to live in fear? Celebrities and top executives fear stepping out of their shells because they don't want to lose what they have. They accomplished something great, and it's uncomfortable to go outside of what you're good at and comfortable with. What they forget is that their initial risk-taking is what got them to be celebrities and top executives! Seeing pressure as a negative thing **keeps us from ever living a life we truly love!**

## TRAGEDY IS THE WORSE PRESSURE OF ALL

I haven't even talked about the most immense pressure point; tragedy. This takes people down so often, but the pressure can create the most remarkable comeback stories. Tragedy is never easy, especially when we haven't done any work to become mentally tough. When you don't have a written plan of action for your life, tragedy will quickly throw you off course.

Divorce is such a typical example of tragedy these days. Just because it's common doesn't make it any better. For men and women around the world, they live their lives to help each other succeed and stay happy. But then, when that "guaranteed" relationship you both committed to at the altar is torn apart, what are you living for?

I see this same thing with athletes. All my young football players would love to play in college and professionally. Other young athletes start as early as five years old with sports like dance, gymnastics, or tennis with these same aspirations. Then, as time goes on, they find that the competition from other kids is brutal, or their family doesn't have the financial means to get them to the professional level. Since a large majority of the very dedicated athletes in this country don't go pro, at some point, they must face this reality and move on. That's tough, in any case!

This is why I always tell my athletes to plan to pursue some other interest. I get it; they want to live the dream and be a star athlete! That sounds awesome to me too! The big news is it's going to end eventually. What other professional interests or talents do you have that you could make a living with? You might use your physical exercise and sport to become a physical trainer or coach or work as a salesperson in the sport you love.

This is why I give such an emphatic message to write down the plan you want for your life. When my sons died, it was so difficult to understand why this would happen. Did this need to happen? Did they really need to die before I did? When I lost my businesses and started selling sporting equipment again in my 50s, it was frustrating to convince myself to keep going.

I could pick myself back up, though, because I had a plan for life! I wasn't just moseying around and hoping good things would happen. I proactively declared what I wanted to take place, and that's why I can look back and say that I didn't fall short under pressure. I didn't cave into the stress. I used this pressure to move forward.

My only advice for getting past tragedy is simply experiencing it. Therapists and psychologists could give you more intelligent answers, but life is just hard. There are some things you can't emotionally prepare for. You could become a cripple one day, lose your job out of the blue, contract a lifelong illness that plagues you, find out your child is addicted to illegal drugs, or have your spouse threaten to leave you. These things happen all the time out of nowhere. We never believe it will happen, but it can.

## MAKE PRESSURE YOUR GREATEST ASSET

The first way to make pressure your greatest asset is by accepting it. Acceptance is necessary for any self-improvement program (like the 5 Stages of Grief or the 12 steps in Alcoholics Anonymous). It's always the most challenging step because it's brutally honest. Telling yourself for the first time that a dear friend is gone forever is never easy. Some people never get over heartbreak and tragedy. They haven't moved on.

It's not just acceptance but also how you react to it. When spouses lose their husband or wife, they can live their lives afterward as a shell of themselves. They are less ambitious and don't have the same passion for making the most out of each day. They put their identity into their spouse's existence and did everything for them.

In contrast, tragedy is how some of the most outstanding non-profit organizations and charities are created. Even if they never blossom to become world-changing organizations, they'll positively impact someone, which counts. By accepting the loss and living your life in an honorable, aspiring manner, you use pressure to your advantage.

I won't belabor the next point because I've mentioned it several times already. Write down the plan and goals to honor this person with your improved life. If you want to create a non-profit to help a community recover from a traumatic loss, what's the plan for making it great? You only figure that out once you write it down.

Another crucial step is to stay active with those you love and who *really* love you. The natural inclination in depression is to be alone and wallow in your sorrow. Whether you lose someone, your business, or your job, a time of mourning is appropriate. You have to accept the fact that this negative thing happened and truly understand the consequences.

This should not be permanent, however. You need to engage with those you enjoy being around. They will be the adequate fuel to re-charge you in your moment of crisis. At the same time, they need to enjoy you too. What's dangerous about tragedy is that it could swing us back to people who were never good to us. This is why in hard times, we are tempted to link back up with former exes and bad friends who end up encouraging us to make harmful decisions. This is also why tragedy often sends us more deeply into our vices.

If you need to talk to someone, don't wait! Talk to your father, your mother, your uncle, your college friend, your high school friend from way back, or that guy who's always nice to you at your haircut place! What you need is someone who will listen and won't judge. They can encourage you and give you the healthy criticism you need to make wise decisions moving forward. Have them help you create a written plan and keep you accountable for the plan. They can help you face the reality of your new life.

With all three of these ingredients, you finally move forward. You utilize pressure by acceptance, a written plan, and friendly support. We've talked about how to create a plan and execute it. We've gone over the 5 P's for building mental toughness, so you know what it takes! Now, it's time to put this into action, no matter what gets in your way, even if it's immensely tragic.

We can't escape life's demands and pressures, but we can be very good at tackling any situation and leveraging it to our advantage. We do this not only for our good but for the benefit of the whole team around us. The pain of loss and disappointment never completely disappears, but with your brazen, written pathway for honoring your tragedy with triumph, you'll have the toughest brains anyone has ever seen.

CHAPTER 10

# A LIFE-LONG JOURNEY TO MENTAL TOUGHNESS

I have travelled a lifelong journey of ups and downs, setbacks, tragedies that I thought I could never overcome. What I found through all of these life experiences is that to achieve, to obtain everything you want out of life, you need to be able to just MOVE FORWARD.

What has happened to you, is your lesson on how to get better and achieve. Don't let the struggles of life define your life. I develop this MOVE FORWARD attitude by defining the 5 P's to develop mental toughness. The ability to move forward under pressure is what life is all about. Learn and master the 5 P's to developing mental toughness and you too can overcome the setbacks that I was dealt in life.

The hardest thing for anyone to do is take action. People spend tons of money hiring business coaches and life coaches, attending seminars and conferences, reading books, and listening to podcasts, all for the pursuit of improvement. Then what happens? Not a lot most of the time. As you now know, it's because people aren't persevering through the initial pains of growth. They don't dig deep to find their passion and progress through all the necessary stages of development.

So for your sake, this is what the last chapter is about. How do we put this into practice? How do we take the 5 P's and the Three Phases of Achievement and make a distinct difference in our lives? It would be a shame if you didn't feel confident that you could genuinely improve your life and find your passion by the end of this book.

I'll create a couple of hypothetical scenarios that will help you see how this whole pursuit of mental toughness is broken down. If lessons are not actionable and practical, then it's just a bunch of empty noise in your brain. That's not unhelpful!

## KARA, THE TENNIS STAR

For our first story, let's say there's a girl named Kara, and like all young boys and girls, she wants to live a remarkable life. She lives in Chandler, Arizona (just outside of Phoenix), and her parents have worked hard to provide the financial means necessary for her to pursue whatever her heart desires. Kara wants to get good at something, like really good. So good that she receives grand honor and professional rewards for that skill. She sees those athletes on television and is amazed at what they can do. She wants to be like them!

First, we must figure out what sport Kara would be passionate about. If she wants to be on the big screen and get professionally paid to play a sport, she must be committed to that sport for a long time. That's difficult for kids because many of them like all kinds of sports. This isn't a bad thing either! Our children should explore their interests to find what truly makes them feel alive. Children are pretty non-committal creatures, usually bouncing around from sport to sport. Plus, if it's a small school she attends, she'll be pressured to participate in volleyball, basketball, track, softball, and any other extracurricular activity the school offers. Small schools are desperate to get anyone and everyone to participate!

Even this early in our development, we are faced with challenges to our mental toughness. Pressure from all sides points us toward activities and passions that *sound fun* but ultimately keep us from the primary goal. The voices that say, "Oh come on! She's just a kid. Let her have fun," are the same voices who never made it professionally and are secretly dream killers. They didn't see it happen to them, so they discouraged other young dreamers from trying.

The options are limited for female athletes to receive professional acclaim too. Female athletes don't have the same appeal as male sports leagues, so we need to be particular here. Basketball is rising in popularity, but most women aren't 6'0," and Kara's parents aren't that tall. So that's likely not the best fit. Soccer is getting much more popular in the United States and could be a good fit. Tennis has always been a great sport for women, but it's a costly sport. Kara could also become a master at an Olympic sport like volleyball, track & field, or downhill skiing, but again, the options are minimal for someone to make a name for themselves in these sports.

Since Kara's family has the financial means, let's say that she picks tennis as her sport. The best athletes in the world started training in their sport before they were ten years old, so she needs to get signed up for tennis lessons immediately. Not only does she need a class, but like many children, Kara learns much more quickly with one-on-one attention from a teacher. Kara's parents also sign her up for private lessons, which are at least $60 per hour. With professional ambitions like Kara, I wouldn't be surprised if the lessons were more expensive. That's on top of the group classes twice a week. And if the parents sign her up with an official tennis gym, the costs could be $1000/month to support her ambition to dominate in tennis.

Kara is having a lot of fun and continues to get better and better. After several years, though, her peers pressure her to participate in other programs, like dance, cheerleading, or acting. She goes to a nice school in the Chandler area, which has many extracurricular activities for children to flourish in. She's begging her parents to go and try out for the cheer squad or next Spring's play. Kara's parents want her to be happy and have fun in multiple activities, but at the same time, it's Kara's dream to be an all-star athlete and compete at the highest levels. Is it the parents' responsibility to ensure she stays on track with her original dream? Is it better to let Kara be a kid and have fun pursuing many interests? These are the tough questions each parent wrestles with.

Since Kara is begging incessantly, her parents allow her to participate in next Spring's play. The problem is that Spring starts many tennis tournaments. These are pivotal events for players to get noticed by great tennis coaches. Even at a young age, like 13 years old, coaches are looking for the next superstar players. Some of the professional athletes in the tennis world start as early as 16 years old. Currently, the youngest player to rank in the top 100 list is Cori "Coco" Gauff. She's 17 years old right now and turned pro back in 2018. That means she's been playing professional matches as early as 14 years old! That's crazy to think about!

A big thing to remember about all-star athletes though is all of them were seen as the "super disciplined" kids growing up. You didn't find them attending tons of social parties because they needed to keep their rest for practices and tournaments. They had friends, but many of them played their same sport.

Coco's an interesting character. Her love for the sport came while watching Serena Williams in the 2009 Australian Open. The way she competed inspired Coco to take a chance with tennis.

She began her first tennis lessons at the age of six years old and honestly disliked practicing. So for the first two years, she did it just to play with friends. When she first started to compete in tournaments though, she found out she was quite good for her age. She won tournaments and seemingly out of nowhere, a great boldness and competitiveness burst out of her. The initial passion found in Serena Williams could be found in this preteen child. From the early tournament days at eight years old, she blazed a ferocious trail toward a dominant young career. She's ranked #12 in the world and if you look her up online, you'll find that as early as 17 years old, she's apparently won almost $2.5 million in total prize money.

Coco's parents had a big part to play in her life, and Kara's parents must also play an important role. Parents are so crucial for the development of remarkable children. It really sets the stage for what kind of life these children will lead as they mature through adolescence, their twenties and beyond. Coco's mom and dad apparently both played college sports, with her father playing basketball at Georgia State University and her mother running track and field at Florida State University. Both Coco's parents were college athletes and had a deep understanding of the value of excelling at sports. This gave her parents the necessary motivations for spending 5-figures per year in the development of Coco's training and traveling for tournaments.

If we look back at Kara's journey, she's now in her early teens and quite good at tennis. She's won local and regional tournaments here and there, but the allure of stage acting and her friends at school keep her attention away from tennis. Plus, after about five years of tennis under her belt, she's getting into the advanced techniques and disciplines of the sport. This is arguably the most frustrating part of anyone's development in a skill.

Robert Greene talks about this stage of development in his book, *Mastery*. In every stage of development in mastering a skill, there's a rift that forms between the skilled novice and the advanced protege. People who become advanced in their trade typically have (1) a close mentor, coach or apprenticeship to specifically train the bright protege, (2) an intense focus that no one can relate to and (3) a grand vision to become a master at the trade. The talented novices fall short from mastery because of the distractions or "pressures" of the world around them. As Robert Greene succinctly sums up,

> *"The time that leads to mastery is dependent on the intensity of our focus."*

So in Kara's story, she continues to be half-hearted in her training. She really enjoys acting, and because of the continued improvement she's seeing, she ends up quitting tennis altogether. The years of practice were fun and will certainly help her understand some important lessons for life. She now knows what it takes to be dedicated to a skill and how important maintaining physical fitness is. She'll likely come back to the sport later in life! A love for something is not so easily forgotten.

In the end, she can't say that she became a professional tennis player like she dreamed as a young child. And while we're creating fictional narratives, let's hypothesize an alternative ending. What if she never quit tennis and still did acting? There would certainly be scheduling conflicts, and the high school life would be grueling, but she'd likely be able to play college tennis. She could go to school for a degree in acting while playing for the school's tennis team. Because she didn't quit tennis, she could work as a tennis instructor at an LA tennis facility. While instructing younger kids, she could spend the off-time auditioning for acting roles. If Kara just stayed in her sport for the long haul, she would have a truly mastered skill to enjoy for the rest of her life.

If we take a closer look at Kara's journey, you'll notice I didn't include some key elements to mental toughness. We don't see her writing down her dreams. We don't see her utilizing a schedule or other practical tools. But honestly, what kid uses a calendar? These skills fall back on the parents to implement. As the adults in Kara's life, she ultimately leans on her parents to have the skills to effectively plan and document the progress for Kara. She can see progress and a passion for the sport, but her parents will be the driving force to motivate her.

The two P's that Kara could have utilized more effectively is perspective and perseverance. She needed the perspective to wisely understand the feedback and pressures around her, and stay on a focused path. While her parents can do what they can to guide her, she must be able to have a clear, unwavering perspective to stay on target for her original, passionate goal. This is also why Robert Greene writes, *"People around you, constantly under the pull of their emotions, change their ideas by the day or by the hour, depending on their mood. You must never assume that what people say or do in a particular moment is a statement of their permanent desires."* Like most people, young and old, Kara changed her mind as she grew up and didn't persevere through the challenges of truly becoming a master.

Now, you might be thinking to yourself, "Coach P, she's just a kid. Do you think it's really healthy to force your children to stay in a sport because 'you know what's best for them?' Wouldn't it be better if they just had fun and enjoyed their childhood?" In this case, I agree with you and support what happened in Kara's life. Kara's parents strongly encouraged her to continue with tennis, but after plenty of efforts, she still wanted to dedicate herself to acting as her main activity. If her parents made her continue with tennis and barred her from acting because of all the money and time they spent getting her good, that's when a child's relationship with their parents tends to go south. You hear stories of resentment and malice toward parents.

What shouldn't be forgotten though is Kara's original commitment. She won't forget that either, especially after all the time and energy spent getting really good as a child. As great parents, you do your best to help your children understand difficult lessons and moral principles. And the moral principle here is to keep your original, honored commitments as long as possible. If Kara just stayed in the sport, she'd be able to find lucrative and fulfilling fruits to enjoy for her entire life from her original passion. But now, it will simply be a hobby that won't provide her much fulfilling purpose. This is a story of a young woman who could've illustrated great mental toughness and perseverance through temporary pain.

## SAM, OLD DOG, CAN LEARN NEW TRICKS

Let's paint another, entirely different picture. Sam is 44 years old and has worked as an auto mechanic his whole life. He's got a wife and three kids, two of his kids are from a previous marriage he had in his early 20's. Sam divorced his first wife before the kids were five years old and he's been paying child support ever since. He's been married to his 2nd wife for almost eight years now and things are okay. Not amazing, but okay. Sam grew up in the suburbs of Detroit and while he really wanted to move out to the Pacific Northwest because of a trip with college friends to Oregon, it wasn't possible for him. Sam's mother ended up contracting cancer while he was in college, so he dropped out of school to support the family. Even after his mother's death, he has since stayed in Detroit.

Sam's parents weren't the most well-off people. A crime-ridden area like Detroit caused their family to have a couple break-ins in their house. That didn't help a father who worked a $50,000 construction job, and a mother who was a substitute teacher at a local school. It was a liveable wage for the family, but definitely not lavish. With all of the problems that come with living in a low-income, Detroit suburb, Sam couldn't explore the kind of opportunities that Kara had in Chandler, Arizona.

Sam going to college was very noteworthy for the family, and a chance for him to make a better life for himself. Once he committed to take care of his mother (which is undoubtedly a great moral decision), it sucked Sam back for good in Detroit. His mother passed away before Sam's 30th birthday, and his father afterwards became slower and slower with his work. Sam's father was eventually laid off and now with Sam's income, he takes care of his father, one child, his 2nd wife and pays child support for two other kids.

This doesn't sound as nice as Kara's story, huh? You might find Sam's story much more relatable actually. Whatever the situation, we're all like Sam in some ways. We all have external pressures and perceptions that can keep us in a lackluster existence. While you may live in a nice neighborhood, you're in a job that doesn't align with your passions. You might have a nice job, but you live in a poor home or have a marriage that's on the brinks. We all have our own pressures and problems. The sooner you realize that we all have our own tough issues, the better you'll be at making friends.

What Sam's life requires is a willingness and tenacity (a mental toughness) to move forward. Thankfully, Sam does more forward. Sam has worked at the same auto shop for over five years and his boss and him have grown close in companionship. Sam, after so many years, finally lets his boss know about the issues going on in his world. His boss listened to him and referred him to Dave Ramsey. After listening to his radio show, Sam reads one of his classic books, *Total Money Makeover,* during a Christmas break. He can't get enough of this guy! He's now hearing an authoritative, wise voice like never before, and it's transforming his perception on life. For the first time, he's getting clear ideas and plans about how to improve his life.

Sam begins to write down goals and ambitions. He confesses these ideas and plans to his wife and to his surprise, she's loving his leadership in making a better family and livelihood. It's like she's more attracted to Sam now because of his improved confidence about life. Who knew women love confident men?

Sam begins saving his money little by little, and chipping away at old credit card debts. Thankfully, he didn't have any student loans because he only went to college for three semesters, but he has piled up several thousands of dollars of credit card debt. Within a year of hardwork and great discipline, Sam's family is free of credit card debt and has saved two months worth of expenses in the bank account. Go Sam!

Sam had to make sacrifices for this to happen. He had to cut expenses, trade-in for a lower quality car and frequently work extra hours at the auto shop to make this reality happen. His wife committed to no longer randomly shopping and she even found a side hustle to help supplement more savings. They also enforced a stricter budget for groceries and child expenses. Sam even committed to sobriety for the last half of the year. The alcohol expenses alone were costing the family a couple hundred dollars a month! During this time, Sam and his wife looked at the bank accounts and credit card statements very frequently. It's as if this was their fascination.

Sam bought into mental toughness. In just one year of 110% commitment, he's on his way to change his family's financial well-being. If we go back to Maslow's Hierarchy of Needs, Sam at the beginning of this story placed constant, critical attention to his Physiological and Safety needs. I mean, he had to, right? As a consequence of his lifestyle choices, he was seen by his wife as another deadbeat guy who just works all day and drinks in the evening. There's no passion for something greater, to lead his family to higher heights!

If he kept living life as he was, I could imagine that his wife might be tempted to notice other potential mates and lose interest in Sam. They would continue to make minimum payments on credit card debts. Lots of things could go south for Sam if he didn't make a change. Sam's work through Dave Ramsey's guidance helped him provide more adequately for his family's needs. This kept the family more secure financially and it even improved his Belongingness because of Sam and his wife's grown connection over changing the trajectory of the family.

When you, the reader, make these same improvements in your life, you'll notice that mental toughness is an exponentially rewarding trait. For Sam, he's now been on the Dave Ramsey kick for three years. He's expanding to other helpful podcasts and reading materials. He's now saved almost $30,000 in his savings bank account. He's also set up a Roth IRA where he sets aside money for retirement.

Sam and his boss continue to become close. Their families go on dates and hangouts together. Sam's boss is very intrigued by his transformation and dedication to living a better life. He's given Sam two raises in the past two years and he's about to drop a bombshell idea. The boss will soon go to Sam and confess that he wants to step away from the business. He wants to, over a five to ten year period, sell the business to Sam and let him manage and grow the auto shop.

These are really exciting times for Sam, and none of it would have happened if he didn't implement the 5 P's. Let's break it down:

- Sam grew **passionate** about improving the trajectory of his family. Because of this, he also grew more passionate about demonstrating excellence everywhere else in his life.
- Sam's whole **perception** of his problems were now positive. He (1) heard testimony after testimony from The Dave Ramsey Show about others who changed their life, (2) wrote down goals and plans on how to achieve this change himself and (3) stayed committed to the plan. His whole mindset is now shifting to someone who's a victor, instead of a victim.
- Sam's **perspective** has also changed to a future of positivity. With this perspective, he becomes a leader to

those around him. He's never thought of himself as a leader, but due to his pursuit of excellence, he's naturally becoming one without him realizing it. Why else would his boss think about passing the business to Sam?

- Sam's **progression** is very clear and obvious because he commits to his plans and tracks the progress. He and his wife have become tight about everything and celebrate the small victories in their marriage and family.
- In the last three years, Sam's **perseverance** has ensured a future life full of breakthroughs like never before.

---

Yes, these were fictitious stories, but you know my story, and you know countless other stories where real mental toughness was demonstrated. It's time for you to get off the bench in life and become the most mentally tough individual you know! To reiterate, here are the steps you can implement right now:

1. **Find out what your passion is.**
2. Break out a sheet of paper or whiteboard and list out anything you enjoy or love.
3. Identify one or two things you want to focus on this year. See what happens.
4. **Write down goals and plans for accomplishing these passions.**
5. Nothing will happen if you don't do this.
6. Track the progress with calendars, to-do lists and journals. Talk with your spouse or close friends regularly about these plans so you have an encouraging circle around you.

7. **Digest books and podcasts to improve your mindset**
8. The perception of how you see things will ensure that you are able to commit to your plans for the long haul.
9. You'll be a more pleasant person by doing this!
10. Listen to my podcast!
11. **Once you achieve goals, pile on and add to them as capable.**
12. **Persevere and never quit.**

## MY LIFE FULFILLING JOURNEY

We all have a journey we're embarking on. After all these years, I've put into bullet points some of the distinct moments in my life.

**My Mental Toughness Journey:**

Age 27: Father dies

Age 28: Younger brother dies

Age 34: lose a teammate of the practice field

Age 35: best friend dies in a motorcycle accident.

Age 36: Brother-in-law passes away, 1st son godmother passes away.

Age 47: 3rd Son (John) passes away (24 years old)

Age 49: Youngest son develops seizures

Age 63: Youngest Son (Joe) passes away from a seizure in his sleep

---

**But hold on, this is a depressing journey full of only the negative moments.** I've had a lot of really great moments of triumph and victory in my life! Here are those distinct moments:

**My Triumphant, Life Fulfilling Journey:**

1972 - Dishwasher in Restaurant, successfully working my first job

1974 - Graduated from High School, become a grocery clerk at Hills Foods in Alsip, Il and met my future wife.

1975 - Stock clerk at Jewel Foods (learned to drink), then became stock clerk at Toy-r-us. Got married too!

1976 - Got hired at Griffith labs and my 1st son was born

1978 - 2nd son born

1980 - 3rd son born

1984 - Semi-Pro football career began (and lasted for seven years); also coached baseball and started a sporting goods business

1986 - Expanded my business to include printing and won the local baseball championship. I had all-star championships for next the six years.

1987 - Became a manager at a local sporting goods retail store

1989 - Began coaching football

1990 - Became salesman for a restoration company and head sophomore football coach for Marist High School

1991 - 4th son is born

1992 - Became head sophomore coach for Prospect High School

1993 - Started my own restoration business and became offensive coordinator for Weber High School

1994 - Became head football coach for Luther High School (5 years after starting)

1996 - Quit drinking (21 years to date) - At 39 years old, I didn't like who I was when I was drinking.

1997 - Started real estate part-time

1998 - Expanded business to include reconstruction and flipping homes. Won my election for Park District Commissioner in my county and became coach of Elmhurst College

2000 - Returned to school to obtain bachelor's degree

2003 - Started my own real estate and property management company. So, I'm a head coach, Park District Commissioner, sober, own a property management company and a construction/restoration company at 46 years old.

2009 - Lost everything in the market crash, in my early 50s

2010 - Began position selling sporting goods and started running political campaigns

2013 - Graduated from college with a Bachelor's degree in Business Management with minor in Marketing - 56 years old, set the goal of being a teacher and head football coach

2014 - Moved to Florida - started & completed my Master's Degree in Education (Educational Leadership). Then, I began to teach Business Education and coach at University High School in Orlando.

2015 - Become the head football coach of University High School at 58 years old. My ideal, dream life is back after just a few years of hardship!

2017 – Went back to school for additional classes to obtain Professional Educators Certification.

---

You have the ability to move forward. Master the 3 phases of achievement Passion - Goal Setting - Mindset and you will live an amazing, motivated, and fulfilling life!

# ABOUT THE AUTHOR

Jim Pusateri (Coach "P") is a teacher, coach, and mentor who helps others develop the Mental Toughness needed to succeed in athletics, life, and business. He is a high school teacher and head football coach at Central High School in Brooksville, Florida. After coaching at various levels over two decades (including college coaching), Jim felt he could make the biggest impact in high school athletics.

> *"It is at this level that you truly can change the course of a student's life."* - Coach Jim Pusateri

Jim has over 30 years of life, business, and athletic coaching experience where he has developed his Mental Toughness Story. He has developed several start-up companies from the ground up and now helps business owners, students, athletes and adults realize that Mental Toughness is the secret to obtaining success and true happiness.

He also hosts the Mental Toughness podcast where every day, he shares a nugget of knowledge with listeners around the world about how they can improve their day just a little bit more, and foster more mental toughness.

"My passion is to educate and inspire people to MOVE FORWARD toward success. **How can I help you develop the Mental Toughness to succeed?"**

---

## WANT MORE FROM COACH JIM PUSATERI?

Jim Pusateri is always looking for new opportunities where he can offer his knowledge, experience, and creativity. If you enjoyed the book so much, there's more to check out that Coach P has to offer! Here are more resources you'll find:

1. His Website: www.inspiringthem.com
2. His Daily Podcast: *The Mental Toughness Podcast with Coach P* (found anywhere you can get podcasts)
3. YouTube: "Coach P – Jim Pusateri"
4. Email: CoachP@InspiringThem.com

www.ingramcontent.com/pod-product-compliance
Ingram Content Group UK Ltd.
Pitfield, Milton Keynes, MK11 3LW, UK
UKHW042017190726
13854UKWH00005B/2332

9 798218 226534